DATA JOURNEY

The ultimate guide for transforming business data into opportunities

Vivek Parate

ISBN: 978-93-95266-31-4 (Paperback)

Any references to historical events, real people, or real places are used fictitiously. Names, characters and places are product of the author's imagination.

Published by: Beeja House

First Printing Edition 2023
Printed By: Repro Books Limited

Author Email: datajourneybook@gmail.com

www.vivekparate.com

Contents

Preface

Each one of us generates an enormous amount of data every day through mobile devices or through social media like Facebook, Instagram or Twitter, or through any digital transactions like online shopping, banking transactions, etc. Organisations use those data to understand business and customer behaviours better. Data Journey addresses all the key processes that involve converting raw data into insight. It deals in detail with the major and latest techniques in each data journey stage, which include data collection, data storage, data transformation, data analysis, and data visualisation. The book contains an overview of different AI/ML, Data mining, and Big Data techniques. It is also helpful to understand data security and governance.

Multiple use cases are included in the topic that will help to understand the importance of particular topics and how industries are solving industrial challenges using the data.

This book can serve as an excellent handbook for researchers and anyone who wants to learn more about the data and everything about the data.

I would be hesitant to call this a complete data journey, but this book covers most of the data intent and journey in the business world.

Who This Book Is For?

While it is true, all of us contribute in generating and consuming data. It is important to understand how we are generating data, and how different organisations are using your data to make better solutions for you and for better business decisions.

The real question is why you should read a long-detailed book on data. The answer is that, if you can or should have influence in generating or consuming data at any point then you should read this book. Data is good for both businesses and users. The business has to set direction to get insight through exploring customers' data and protecting important customer data. This book helps you to understand the technical aspects of getting data into insight.

On the business side, those who have a piece of special knowledge and interest in at least one of the key aspects of the data journey (data storage, data transformation, data exploration, data visualisation, data security and governance) should find this book very useful.

Finally, C-level executives should be aware of the breadth and scope of the data journey (data to insight). In reality, C-level executives create analytic strategies without knowing much about the overall process. This book will help C-level executives with all the key elements involved when thinking about analytic and data protection strategies.

Those who interact with businesses regarding some aspect of data should also find the book of interest.

In addition, this book is an excellent handbook for researchers and anyone who wants to learn more about the data and everything about the data.

Acknowledgement

I would like to thank all the people who helped me, either directly or indirectly, in the preparation of this book. Your knowledge, wisdom, and support has been (and is) invaluable in advancing my research.

However, while I would like to identify each of you by name, I feel that I need to single out those who have been supportive and helpful over years for special acknowledgement. Kudos are deserved by:

- Santosh Parate
- Anil Wadhai
- Sagir Mohd
- Kaushik Dey

And last but not least, my very supportive wife, Rina, and lovely son Kabir

One

Data is Everywhere

Everyone of us generates data starting from our birth certificates and continues till our death certificates and beyond.

Introduction to Database

In today's world, databases are such an integral part of our day-to-day lives that we are not even aware that we are using them or generating them. From our birth to death, we consume and generate data. The trail of data starts with the birth certificate and continues all the way to the death certificate and beyond. In between, each individual produces or consumes enormous amounts of data.

The word data is a plural form of the Latin word "datum", which means "things given". Data is the interface between you and the rest of the world. Each one of us interacts and exchanges data in our daily activities. We understand our society, our body, our economy, banking etc in the form of data. Everything you see around us is one form of data. We interact with data every day.

In the technical world, data can be defined as a representation of facts, concepts, or instructions in a formalised manner, which should be suitable for communication, interpretation, or processing by human or electronic machines.

Data can be expressed in two forms: quantitative or quantitative.

Quantitative data represents data that can easily be measured or quantified, such as the stock market up by 2% today or the global average median age was 30 years in 2021.

Qualitative data represent opinions or feelings and cannot be represented by a numerical statistic such as an average.
E.g. animals can sense unusual activities, a good journalist can surface truth with their set of questions etc.

Example:

"If a survey asked 300 respondents the question, "Do you like watching films?"

Responses could be "Yes" or "No". Let's assume 210 responded "Yes" and 90 responded "No", it can be converted into percentages as 70% of which is a quantitative fact.

If you ask another follow-up question with an open-ended "Which characters do you like more and why? Response to this question would vary depending upon the nature of persons and like, and dislike. These descriptive insights cannot easily be quantified into numbers, so they are qualitative.

Quantitative	Qualitative
70% of survey respondents are watching movies on a regular basis.	"I like the Marvel series the most, my favourite character is Iron Man"
On average 10-12 hrs in a month people generally spend time watching movies.	"I like Thriller movies a lot and generally, I watch them after midnight"
25-30 years of age range generally has more inclination toward romantic movies.	Online ticket booking is more convenient than standing in a queue.

A Day in the life of Your Data

Data is a magical word and it is a bigger part of our life. From our mobile devices to card payments to the Internet of things, data is growing exponentially, 2.5 quintillion bytes per day.

The 9th edition of "Data Never Sleeps" provides a glimpse of how much data is created every digital minute in our increasingly data-driven world. Reports say that as of July 2021, 65% of the world population accesses the internet which is almost 10% more than in early 2021. It is expected that the data would grow to over 180 zettabytes by 2025, compared to 2021 which was 79 zettabytes. The table below shows some data.

Data generated in a minutes

Source - data-never-sleeps-9 infographics

Let's understand how much data you generate in a day with an example of Priya's life. Most of you would share the same life activities as Priya, you can imagine yourself in the same situation and find out what your generated data looks like.

Priya Morning Walk with her friends

It's 6:00 am in the morning and Priya is planning for a morning walk with her friend Anna. Before talking to Anna, Priya opens up a weather app for weather prediction and temperature for the next 1-2 hours on her smartphone. She checked her calendar just to confirm no early meeting invites. Once she found everything was ok, she dialled Anna and planned her morning walk route. During her morning walk planning, she opened up 3 apps, weather apps, google calendar and google maps. Priya's current location information is captured by those apps along with activities.

Priya uses her smartwatch for her health and steps count

Priya is health conscious and she is very particular about monitoring her health. She uses a smartwatch for her morning walk and throughout the day. Her smartwatch provides health status like heart rates, calories burn, total steps and sleep patterns. Smartwatches transmit health data to a remote server. The remote server keeps Priya's daily activity data and generates alters if it is alarming.

A stop for juice on way to walk

On the way, Priya and Anna generally take healthy herbal juices. Priya pays for juice using her debit card. This payment transaction adds more digital information to her digital world like the location at which she paid, shop information, how much she paid, her favourite juices etc.

Priya and Anna take selfies at the park

Later Priya and Anna take a selfie outside the garden. They play with a photo filter app, settling on adding bunny ears to the photo. The filtering app, however, is able to access all the photos on the device and the attached metadata, rather than only the garden selfie. Priya posts the picture on a social media app. The app links Priya's current online activity to a trove of data collected by other apps, such as his demographic information and purchasing habits, using an email address, a phone number or an advertising identifier.

Songs from Spotify

After returning back to home, Priya decides to have smoothie music so she opens music apps from her smartphone. She plays romantic 90's music. The music app gathers all Priya's activity events, identifies which songs Priya played, which one is her favourite and identifies her mood. The music app understands her choice of music and offers similar music as a new playlist.

Priya checks her emails

Priya thought to check her business and personal emails, she opened the mail app on her mobile and replied to 5-6 emails and composed 4-5 new emails. Priya got an auto-response text while drafting her mail. She is happy because she doesn't need to think too much and it was easy for her.

Time to buy something

Priya loves to do online shopping. Amazon is her favourite site. She likes amazon's recommendation options, but most of the time Priya finds items in recommendations that are more relevant and the same as what she was looking for. Recommendation helps her to make fast decisions without scanning the entire app.

Surprise Notification on 20% discount

Priya and her friend were discussing their next vacation in Kerala. She did some search on google about Kerala. Surprisingly, Priya got some notifications on her mobile from different travel agents and airlines on interesting packages on Kerala trips and a 20% discount on hotel accommodations and flight tickets. She was surprised.

Alexa booked a ride

"It's 10:30 am, time for the office. Would you like to book a ride?" a voice from Alexa. Priya replied

"Alexa, book a Uber cab at 11:30 AM"

Alexa responded back, sure, the cab is booked for the office. Alexa understands Priya's office activities and patterns.

A message that spoils everything

While Priya getting ready for her office, she got a message, she was shocked *"Your XXBank A/C has been debited with INR 80000 on 21-Sept-2022 at 10:40 AM, your available balance is INR 0.00'*

Priya was shocked and fainted for some time....

Priya has generated active and passive data throughout the day. Active data are those where she was knowingly generating data like card payment, posting photos on social media email data etc. Passive data is a kind of data indirectly generated during activities. E.g. data captured by other apps, tracking Priya's live location while walking, Priya's current location tracking while in payment.

Traditionally we think property, plants, equipment, inventory and even human resources are considered key business assets. The explosion of technology over the last decade has made us rethink what valuable assets are. In today's modern world, data is the key for any innovation and business expansions and considered the most valuable asset.

Data is rapidly growing, technological evaluation includes increased internet access, broadband access, mobile phone use, and social media use are driving factors for data growth. Each organisation is trying to capture as much data as it can. What matters most for business is not the volume of data but rather, knowing how to use it. Organisations understand that data is an enterprise asset and has the potential to disrupt market trends.

Today, Companies gather data with multifold intentions that help businesses to understand customers' behaviour patterns and new business opportunities. Whatever data you are generating are stored, transformed and analysed by the company and utilised in business growth.

How does data improve your experiences?

Data is considered a potential source of learning for business. If companies use customer information in the right way they can make better decisions for their business and for improving customer service.

For example, Amazon collects personal data through browser history, purchase history or product searches on websites and suggests items to purchase using predictive analytics. It could be useful to that person certainly, the pop-ups and collected data behind them are useful to Amazon and other online retailers if the suggested items are purchased.

Amazon - Recommendation

Amazon was founded in 1994 by Jeff Bezos and is considered the largest online marketplace in the world in terms of revenue and market capitalization, and the largest internet company in the world in terms of revenue.

Amazon deploys recommendation systems across a number of its services, including its e-commerce platform and its streaming platform.

Recommended For You

Clicking on the "Your Recommendations" link on Amazon.com leads users to a page full of products recommended just for you. Amazon recommends a range of products from different categories you've been browsing, with the aim of putting products in front of you that you're likely to click, learn more about and buy.

Frequently Bought Together

This recommendation has one main goal: increase average order value. 'Frequently bought together' recommendations aim to up-sell and cross-sell customers by providing product suggestions based on the items in their shopping cart or below products they're currently looking at on-site.

Your Recently Viewed And Recommendation Inspired By Your Browser History

Here Amazon looks at products you've been browsing and recommends very similar products of different shapes, sizes and brands to help you find something very similar to a product you've already shown an interest in. They throw different brands, colours, shapes and sizes at you with the hope that they'll place one product in front of you that you cannot resist.

Your Browsing History

If you've already looked at a product, it means you were slightly interested and Amazon knows it, so they'll show you your browsing history in case you want to quickly go back and buy something you previously showed an interest in.

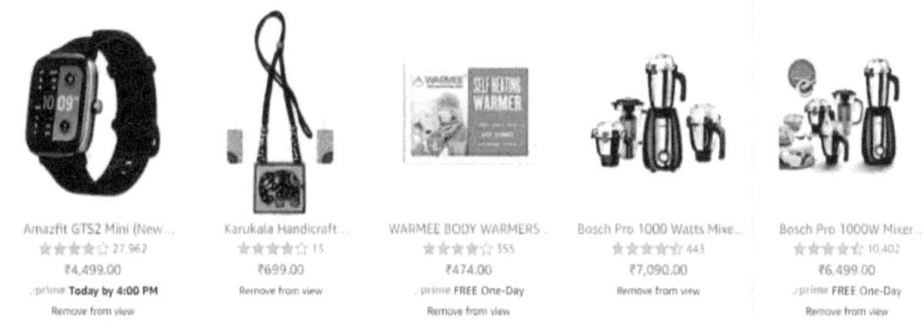

Customers Who Bought This Item Also Bought

Similar to frequently bought together, Amazon displays items that have been purchased together in the past, with the goal to increase average order value through up-sells and cross sells. My guess is that these items are purchased together a little less often than 'frequently bought together' and is a way for Amazon to sell items that are not as popular to help retailers move their inventory.

BUY IT AGAIN

Amazon displays items that you have brought past and might be interested in buying it again.

There Is A Newer Version Of This Item

People love to upgrade their gadgets to the latest version and this recommendation appeals to that need. If I look at the old Kindle I bought on Amazon.com, there is a recommendation underneath the invoice letting me know there is a newer version of the product that I can upgrade to. It's almost like a replenishment campaign but for an electronic device

Amazon's e-commerce recommendation engine is powerful, and it engages with users at every stage of their journey on the website. Amazon recommendation algorithms start by finding a set of customers whose purchased and rated items overlap the user's purchased and rated items. The algorithm aggregates items from these similar customers, eliminates items the user has already purchased or rated, and recommends the remaining items to the user. There are three common approaches to solving the recommendation problem: traditional collaborative filtering, cluster models, and search-based methods.

How does data help to make life easy?

Data helps uncover your pattern and based on the insight from the data, it helps to automates certain services that would ease daily life.

Gmail - Smart Compose

Google announced Smart Compose, a new feature powered by artificial intelligence, to help you draft emails from scratch, faster. Smart Compose suggests complete sentences in your emails so that you can draft them with ease. Because it operates in the background, you can write an email like you normally would, and Smart Compose will offer suggestions as you type. When you see a suggestion that you like, click the "tab" button to use it.

Smart Compose helps save you time by cutting back on repetitive writing, while reducing the chance of spelling and grammatical errors. It can even suggest relevant contextual phrases. For example, if it's Friday it may suggest "Have a great weekend!" as a closing phrase.

Smart, compose personalised suggestions are tailored to the way you normally write, to maintain your writing style. Only you see your own private, personalised suggestions for your account. No other users, including administrators for your organisation, can see your personalised suggestions.

How does data help to save your Life?

Data is life saving if it is used with the right purpose. In the healthcare system , your data is used for more research that would help to reduce costs of treatment, predict outbreaks of epidemics, avoid preventable diseases, and improve the quality of life in general.

Apple watch saves Life

Smart watches are life saving devices that have saved the lives of countless people.we have heard several anecdotes of Apple Watch

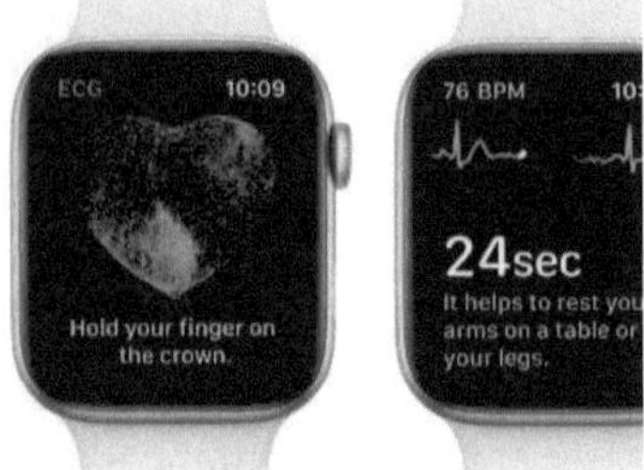

making an early diagnosis of a life-threatening disease, or calling health authorities in times of emergencies, when the patient was unconscious, and the smart watch continues to do its 'life saving' job with due diligence it seems.

The Apple Watch saved the life of a dentist named Nitesh Chopra, a resident of Haryana's Yamuna Nagar, India. Chopra experienced chest pains, and on conducting an ECG with his Apple Watch on March 12, the doctor learned that he had 99.9% blockage of artery.

He quickly went to the doctor, and eventually had a stent installed in his heart through surgery, and returned home safely, after a short stay at the hospital. The doctor's wife, Neha, who had received the watch as a gift a year ago, said that she feels lucky that they had the watch. The watch had been giving indications that Chopra had arrhythmia for a while, however, the couple ignored the signs because they assumed that since Chopra is a young man in his 30s, he would not be prone to such a heart disease.

Another incident, Gabe Burdett from Washington was waiting for his father Bob at a meeting point, from where the two were to go mountain biking together. Burdett instead received a text from his father's Apple watch, saying it detected a fall. The watch provided his father's location too. However, by the time Burdett reached the spot, his father was missing. A startled Burdett gets another text from the same watch, letting him know that his dad had reached the Sacred Heart Medical Center safely.

Burdett got another update from the Watch saying his location has changed with a map location of SHMC. Burdett's dad flipped his bike at the bottom of Doomsday, hit his head and was knocked out until sometime during the ambulance ride.

"If you own an Apple Watch, set up your hard fall detection, it's not just for when you fall off a roof or a ladder," Burdett further explained in his post.

The watch had smartly notified the respective authorities of the accident by calling 911 and emergency medical services were able to reach Bob, who had suffered a head injury, within 30 minutes.

This case is one of several recent cases where Apple watches have helped save lives.

How does data change Sports?

"Sports are watched by millions and millions of people – yet, pretty much all of the strategic decisions are made by humans in a split second. These decisions could definitely be enhanced by learning from past data, but humans can't keep large databases in their heads. Thus, predictive analytics tools will help teams make these decisions. If we know, for instance, that in certain circumstances, a particular coach on the opposition team tends to make a particular decision, then we can be ready for it. We can place sensors all over a car while it is in training for a race, and use the sensor data to help a driver learn how to race better."- said Cynthia Rudin, associate professor of statistics at MIT.

Coaches in professional sports have more technology at their fingertips than ever before. Today, it is possible to track virtually every aspect of an athlete's fitness, training and performance.

Arsenal - Case Study - Firstbeat's 2018 HRV Summit.

Tom Allen is the lead sports scientist at Arsenal FC.His role at the Premier League club involves monitoring and practically applying data to on-field conditioning for the first-team squad. Using Firstbeat Sports' heart rate variability (HRV) data alongside GPS, wellness questionnaires and more, Arsenal cover all the bases when it comes to monitoring the squad throughout the season. Inevitably, this level of in-depth analysis means Allen and Arsenal's support staff receive thousands of data points daily on each member of the team.

The main objective for data collection was "***Reduce injury risk and enhance physical performance.***"

Process: Data are collected on five categories and majored on the scale of 1ot 5 scales for individual players.

- Skeleton stress (stress on the skeleton through speed/distances)
- Metabolic (Acceleration/deceleration)
- Cardiovascular (Heart rate analysis through Firstbeat variables)
- Neuromuscular (how the muscles are responding)
- Psychological (the athlete's wellness)

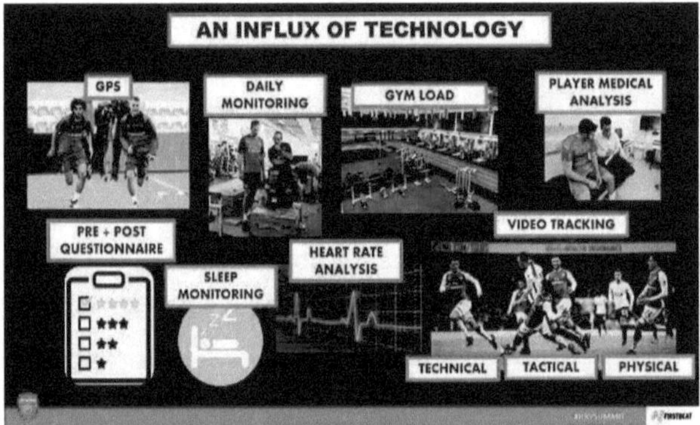

Each category's 1-5 score is created by inputting approximately 75 variables into an algorithm. These category scores are then put through another algorithm to produce a single daily stress score.This process allows Allen and his colleagues to see each player's risk of injury and chance of peak performance at any given time throughout the season.

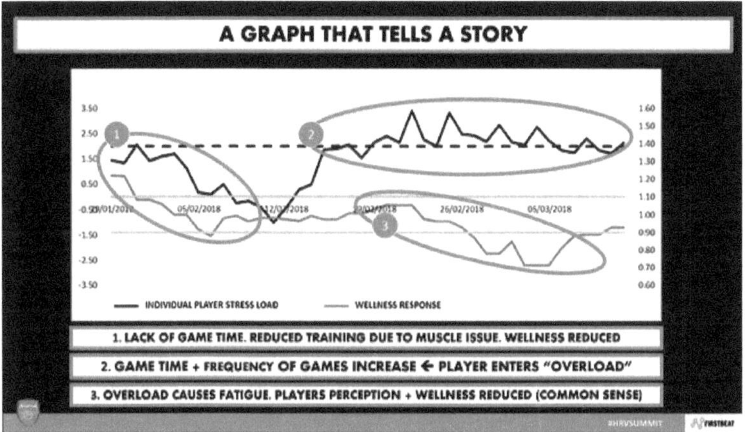

Allen revealed one example of such a graph and how it informed them on a player's situation throughout February 2018.

Stage One – Player is complaining about an ankle issue so training load is reduced. Wellness score also drops as he is reporting more soreness.

Stage Two – By mid-February, there is a gradual increase in load and wellness as the player returns to the training and game environment. However, due to the high frequency of games at this time, the player enters a state of overload.

Stage Three – This overload causes wellness to drop. Under more load and stress, there is a reduction in readiness, increase in soreness and reduction in ability to produce movements in screening profile.

The graph of each player provides actionable data for each player.

Action with Data
Arsenal turns this data into actionable with PMI strategy (P- Protect | M- Maintain | I-Increase)

P (protect): Individuals who are either at increased risk of injury or in a state of overload. These players would not be pushed physically during training due to overload and poor wellness combination.

M (Maintain) – Have experienced a previous state of overload. Could prolong the recovery phase before pushing hard.

I (Increase) – No state of overload in recent weeks. It is possible to push these players hard due to freshness.

Taking a player in the 'I' group as an example, Allen looked at the underlying data. Reviewing the five stress categories, they can design a training plan based around which areas need working on. For example, high speed runs with reduced work:rest ratio are added to the week's plan for a central defender with low skeletal and cardiovascular stress scores. If work on the neuromuscular category is also required, then these runs would take place when fatigued.

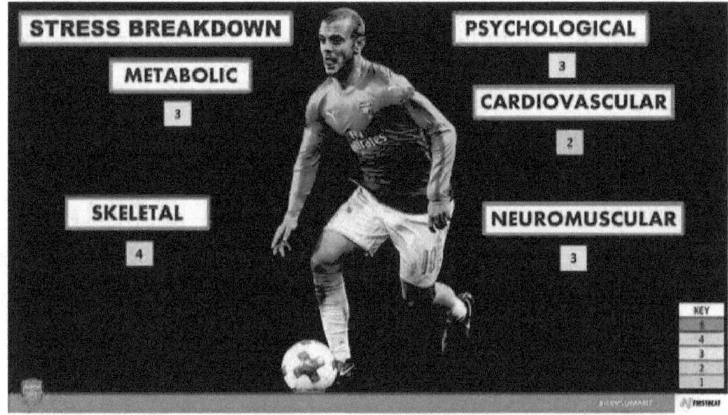

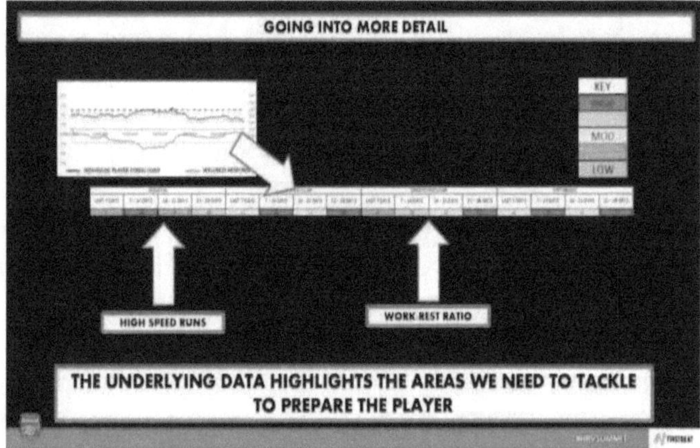

Source - https://www.firstbeat.com/en/blog/how-arsenal-manage-player-data-to-achieve-peak-performance/

Bad guys are around

With demand in data, everyone in the world is behind the capturing or stealing of data for their own interest. Cybercrime is the greatest threat to every company in the world, and one of the biggest problems with mankind. Criminals take advantage of this online transformation to target weaknesses in online systems, networks and infrastructure. There is a massive economic and social impact on governments, businesses and individuals worldwide.

Phishing, ransomware and data breaches are just a few examples of current cyberthreats, while new types of cybercrime are emerging all the time. Cybercriminals are increasingly agile and organised – exploiting new technologies, tailoring their attacks and cooperating in new ways.

The impact on society is reflected in the numbers.

Pune Citibank Mphasis Call Center Fraud

It is a case wherein 2005, US $3,50,000 was transferred from the Citibank accounts of four customers residing in the US. This amount was dishonestly transferred through the internet to the bogus accounts in the US. Some employees of a call centre gained the confidence of the customers from the US. By gaining the confidence of those customers they obtained their PIN disguises as a helping hand to those customers to come out of difficult situations. Later, these numbers were used in committing the fraud.

Call centres in India use the highest security. The employees there are checked whenever they go in and out; to prevent the employees from copying down the account numbers. Therefore, the employees must have memorised the number and went to the cyber café; immediately after leaving the office and accessed the accounts of the Citibank customers.

The accounts were then opened in Pune and the money got transferred into those accounts. Later, the customers complained about their money being transferred to the accounts in Pune and then the criminals got traced.

The service they used to transfer the funds was SWIFT i.e., Society for Worldwide Interbank Financial Telecommunication. When the bank accounts were made in Pune, fake email accounts were also made. The original account holders never received the confirmations which they would have received during the transferring of funds.

 In March 2005, the money was being moved to a dozen bank accounts which were made with the help of two ICICI home loan agents whose role was to facilitate those illegal accounts. They were the non-BPO employees and also among the people who were arrested. Citibank had no idea of the transactions being made until one account holder of Citibank complained.

This fraud raised many kinds of concern which includes the role of "Data Protection". This crime was committed using the unauthorised access to the electronic account space of the customers.

Let's have another example of data exposed.

Almost 100,000 Australians' private details exposed in attack on Westpac's PayID

The private details of almost 100,000 Australian bank customers have been exposed in a cyber-attack on the real-time payments platform PayID, which allows the instant transfer of money between banks using either a mobile number or email address.

This vulnerability made it possible for hackers to execute an enumeration attack - when brute force techniques are used to either confirm or guess valid records in a database.

When the attack was over, the hackers uncovered the banking details of 98,000 Westpac customers.

What data was compromised.
- Full names
- Email addresses
- Phone numbers
- Account information

Armed with these details, cybercriminals can keep retargeting victims with a broad range of phishing attacks.

Know more about Data - DIKW Pyramid

DIKW (Data, Information, Knowledge, Wisdom) explains the distinct relationship between, data, knowledge ,information and wisdom. Data is a foundation for knowledge and wisdom. With increase in the volume of data, will help to grow knowledge and wisdom.

DIKW

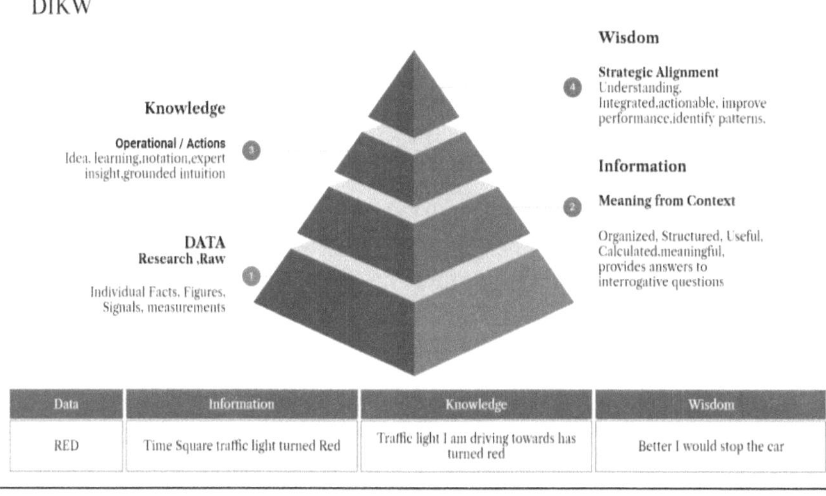

Data	Information	Knowledge	Wisdom
RED	Time Square traffic light turned Red	Traffic light I am driving towards has turned red	Better I would stop the car

Data : With digital evolution, enormous amounts of data is generated and stored every day. Electronically stored data is collected from countless sources, ranging from phone calls, emails, and twitter feeds, to IoT devices, internet clicks and routine pings on a cellular phone for a person's location. This readily available data can tell us more about you or anyone who generates data. By looking Priya's data we can figure out her activities and patterns like:

- She getup early in morning for walk 6:30 AM (Location services)
- She use to take juice at Juice centre (Payment process)
- She like to visit park (Selfies upload at park, photo capture log, lat)
- Her favourite songs includes 90's romantic songs (Spotify capture music played)
- She generally starts office at 10:30AM (Alexa keeps this information)

Information: Commonly defined as the facts provided or learned about something or someone. Information is contained in descriptions, answers to questions that begin with such words as who, what, when and how many. Information systems generate, store, retrieve and process data. Information is inferred from data.

Knowledge: "How" is the information, derived from the collected data, relevant to our goals? "How" are the pieces of this information connected to other pieces to add more meaning and value? And, maybe most importantly, "how" can we apply the information to achieve our goal?

When we don't just view information as a description of collected facts, but also understand how to apply it to achieve our goals, we turn it into knowledge. This knowledge is often the edge that enterprises have over their competitors. As we uncover relationships that are not explicitly stated as information, we get deeper insights that take us higher up the DIKW pyramid.

But only when we use the knowledge and insights gained from the information to make proactive decisions, we can say that we have reached the final – 'wisdom' – step of the Knowledge Pyramid.

Wisdom is the ability to increase effectiveness. Wisdom is the top of the DIKW hierarchy and to get there, we must answer questions such as 'why do something' and 'what is best'. In other words, wisdom is knowledge applied in action.

We can also say that, if data and information are like a look back to the past, knowledge and wisdom are associated with what we do now and what we want to achieve in the future.

DIKW		Intention	Example
Data	Know Nothing	Symbols, figures	$1200
Information	Know What	Data that are processed to be useful; provides answers to who, what, where and when questions	Priya monthly spend $1200 on online shopping from Amazon
Knowledge	Know How	Application of data and information; answers how questions	Priya mostly spends 70% of the amount on traditional dress.
Wisdom	Know Why	Evaluated understanding	Amazon recommend and suggest best traditional dresses to Priya

How is your data journey in industry?

Data generated by you is used in multiple layers, industries use your data to improve product services, understand you better and use this information for business success.

Many industries are rushing to transform their business operations into the digital world. With this digital technology adoption enormous amounts of data are generated every day. There is so much data generated every day that it would be difficult to track without proper strategy. Without proper data strategy, data cannot be converted into any valuable assets. Data needs to be accessible, comprehensible and usable by business strategists for business values.

Process of making data as an asset goes through multiple facets and strategies. Each layer of process is important for refining data into information to knowledge. Data strategy should cover following steps to

- Data Collection
- Data Storage
- Data Transformation
- Data Exploration
- Data Visualization
- Data Protection
- Data Governance

Data Collection: Billion of us are interacting with each other through Word Wide Web, Mobile or other key devices. Collecting the right set of data is crucial for business. There could be multiple sources of collecting data and each source might have its own way of defining data so it's important to have reliable, durable and quality data.

In Chapter -2 we will discuss more detail on data collection.

Data Storage: In Priya's example, Priya generated two kinds of data. In her Facebook post she uploaded a Photo and commented on the post, such data are categorised as unstructured data whereas her online shopping activities mostly under structured data. Unstructured data consist of video, images , free text ,audio etc.Structured data are well in tabular form. So data storage differs depending upon types of data system generating. For Structured-Unstructured, it would be different types of databases and storages. In chapter -3 we will cover more on Data Storage options and Database selection process.

Data Transformation: Data which system collected and stored are totally crude form. It could be fit for system running but might be unfit for data exploration. For Data exploration, data might be collected from multiple sources, it could be internal data or external data. Data transformation is the process of eliminating unnecessary information, clear up unwanted information, validation data, and converting in common data definition.

Data Exploration and Analytic: With increase in Cloud adoption, cost of storing data is drastically reduced with more scalable and reliable options. Storage is so chief each organisation generating a large amount of data that could provide **actionable insights**.

Data exploration is the first step of data analysis used to explore and visualise data to uncover insights from the start or identify areas or patterns to dig into more. Using interactive dashboards and point-and-click data exploration, users can better understand the bigger picture and get to insights faster.

Data Visualization: Is the process of encoding your data into well formatted and understandable format. In this chapter we will talk more on different kinds of data visualisation tools and techniques, important for dashboards.

Data Protection: In April 2021, the personal information of 533 million Facebook users was found posted online by a hacker, including names, birthdays, phone numbers, locations, and email addresses. According to

Facebook, the stolen data had been originally scrapped a few years ago due to a vulnerability that the company patched in 2019.

As we discussed, data is an asset then it is obvious everyone in the world likes to have control or gain on a dataset.The way things are going, the question is not if a breach will happen, but when. Data theft is incredibly lucrative and that makes it a worthwhile endeavour for bad actors to continue to innovate how it is done.

Since 2018, this has been subject to the EU's General Data Protection Regulation (GDPR). Most internet users will have noticed on their first visit to a website a pop-up banner that asks for their "consent" or to "accept cookies"; that's GDPR in action. The idea is that businesses need to justify what they do with personal data, so they must ask you before they track your behaviour online and sell some version of your information to others.

Under Data Protection we will discuss more on Data Resilience which includes 5 main facets:

- Environmental Risk
- Operational Risk
- Cyber Risk
- Application Risk

Data Governance: Digital transformation can make organisations more agile, efficient and customer-centric. While these benefits are well understood, businesses that neglect the governance aspect of digital transformation risk contravening data privacy and security regulations – something no business can afford to do.

Data governance has traditionally been viewed in terms of complying with regulations that stipulate how data must be collected, stored and processed. But AI has introduced new challenges and risks to be managed. It's not enough to obtain a vast amount of data; you also need to consider its characteristics. Where is it coming from? What does it actually represent? Is there anything that you need to account for before feeding this material into your algorithm? Will it train the algorithm in the right things?

How to read this book

Data needs to travel multiple stages to become a useful asset. Companies need a complete end to end solution that lets them manage, aggregate, explore and visualise data, as well as one to help reduce cyber and compliance risk.

This book helps you to provide a basic overview of all those important stages. We called this as a journey from raw data to knowledge, to insight. From insecure to secure and journey from data to business opportunities. Book is going to cover technical and non technical aspects of each stage. We have covered some important real time use cases to explain sections. You can start reading this book from any chapter based on your interest.

Summary

- The word data is a plural form of the Latin word "***datum,***" which means the "things given".

- Data is the interface between you and the rest of the world.

- Data can be defined as a representation of facts, concepts, or instructions in a formalised manner, which should be suitable for communication, interpretation, or processing by human or electronic machine.

- Knowingly or unknowingly, each one of us generates and shares data with many companies.

- Data can be shared for better mankind and reduce uncertainty.

- Amazon recommendation and predictive logic supports a better and fast decision process.

- IPhone (Smartwatches) helps to save our lives in many ways.

- Arsenal Case Study explained how data changes traditional sports into technology friendly.

- DIKW pyramid provides answers to many questions like, **Data** - collection of symbols and figures, **Information** - provides answers to who, what, where and when question, **Knowledge** - Explain on how part mainly application of data and information; **Wisdom** - Evaluated understanding and helps to optimise the experiences.

- From data to knowledge is multifacet steps from collecting raw data into data analysis, to data visualisation. It also talks about how data protection and governance are critical for the entire data journey.

References

- https://www.raconteur.net/technology/data-analytics/data-privacy-and-the-future-of-healthcare/
- https://www.raconteur.net/business-strategy/leadership/digital-transformation-three-priorities-for-governance-leaders/
- https://www.raconteur.net/technology/data-governance-ai-machine-learning/
- https://www.rejoiner.com/resources/amazon-recommendations-secret-selling-online
- https://www.blog.google/products/gmail/subject-write-emails-faster-smart-compose-gmail/
- https://economictimes.indiatimes.com/magazines/panache/apple-watch-saves-haryana-dentists-life-by-detecting-99-9-artery-blockage-ceo-tim-cook-reacts/articleshow/90319891.cms?from=mdr
- https://www.deccanchronicle.com/technology/in-other-news/240919/apple-watch-saves-bikers-life-after-accident.html
- https://www.interpol.int/en/Crimes/Cybercrime
- http://www.cyberlawclinic.org/casestudy.htm
- https://bnwjournal.com/2020/07/17/pune-citibank-mphasis-call-center-fraud/
- https://www.smh.com.au/business/banking-and-finance/australians-private-details-exposed-in-attack-on-westpac-s-payid-20190603-p51u2u.html
- https://www-public.imtbs-tsp.eu/~gibson/Teaching/Teaching-ReadingMaterial/Rowley06.pdf
- https://www.firstbeat.com/en/hrv-summit-2018/

Two

Collect right data

*Scientists do not collect data randomly and utterly comprehensively. The data they collect are only those that they consider *relevant* to some hypothesis or theory.*

– David Lewis-Williams

Introduction

In the last chapter, we discussed more on how data is important in your life, and knowingly unknowingly, we all generate enormous amounts of data every day. As an individual, data helps us make better decisions, for a better quality of life, and for life-saving research and data also helps us to think differently besides traditional approaches.

Many industries are moving towards digital transformation. This digital transformation is a more data-centric approach. This chapter helps you to understand what are the different types of data source an individual and organisation uses to capture this data. This chapter also covers the principles of data collection and data protection.

What are different data sources for you?

If you carefully observe your life, most of the generated data is either through devices or human generated. Take a glimpse of Priya's life again, and you will find, different kinds of data are produced at different events.

Priya's day in a life of data

Priya's morning starts with checking her mobile device, interacting with multiple apps and then she starts her morning walks with a smartwatch on her wrist. Throughout the day she exchanges her data in multiple apps or websites or communicates with devices.
Here are small list of her activities

	Activities	Data Source Type	Data
	Priya checks her emails before walks	Human= generated	Email information and Metadata
	Priya checks Weather before calling Anna	Human-generated	Apps tracked her location
	Priya uses smart watch for morning walk	Device generated Data	Device capture her current location and tracked her health data
	Priya did Card payment on juice shop	Device generated	Card information captured during transaction
	Priya and Anna took selfie and post on social media	Human and device generated	Social media app requested access to all photos, automatically capture geographic location
	Priya did shopping through Amazon sites	Human Generated	Amazon capture transaction data and activities information

As a individuals data are generated mainly in three sources
- Human Generated
- Device generated
- Passive Data

Human Generated Data

Human-generated data consists of the emails, Word documents, spreadsheets, presentations, images, audio, and video files that we create and share with other people every day. Human generated content is huge, and its metadata is even bigger. We will cover this topic in the section below.

It has two categories of intentionally created data and passively created data sometimes called metadata

- **Intentionally created Data**: are those data that are deliberately generated with your own activities and you know you are doing it. In short, data is generated with the help of human actions.

  e.g. upload image, video, text, or audio recordings on social networking sites. When you do web searches records of your web search or keywords are bookmarked. Your email, text messages, online purchases, and bank transactions.

  Within the last 2 years, 90% of data was created, and 70% of data is generated from social media. Social Media is not only a source of human-generated data, every year humans generate a large amount of media and publications.

  - 2.2 million ebook published every year
  - 2 million blogs posted every year
  - 250+ billion email data generated every year

- **Metadata:** Metadata is data about data. You might call it second order of human-generated data. You are generating this data but you are not aware of this information. Sometimes, metadata holds more information than an actual piece of data. In some use cases, metadata is more significant than actual data, especially in the big data world.

  Photo Metadata: For instance, if you take a picture with your phone, along with the picture you get a lot of information with EXIF data (Exchangeable Image File Format).

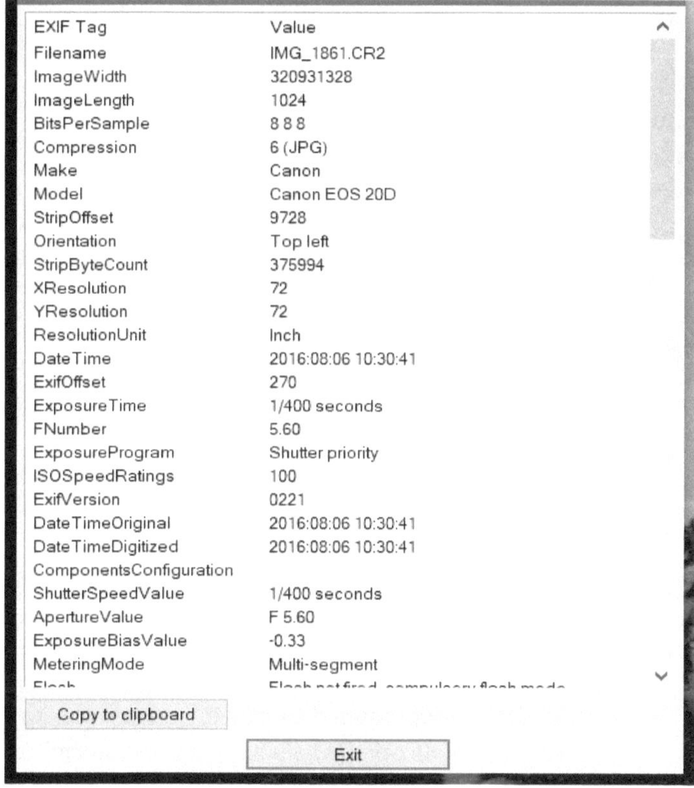

Aside from the name of the file you see the size of the file, the time it has taken, GPS altitude, latitude, longitude and positions.

This is an enormous amount of information you get while you are taking pictures.

Machine Data

Machine data is automatically generated, either as a response to a specific event or a fixed schedule. It means all the information is developed from multiple sources such as smart sensors, medical devices and wearables, road cameras, IoT devices, satellites, desktops, mobile phones, industrial machinery, etc. These sources enable companies to track consumer behaviour.

Machine generated data includes sensor data, machine-generated logs information or any kinds of reports etc.

OnKol Health Hub Designed to Collect Health Information on Your Loved Ones

Hardware startup OnKol has created a device that will help you make sure your loved ones on the other side of the country are in good health.

It provides a team approach to helping care for a loved one, while allowing them to continue to live independently in their home.

- OnKöl simultaneously notifies selected family members and other caregivers of everything from vital signs to incoming and outgoing calls to emergency or panic situations.

- OnKöl can be programmed to provide a reminder to the user to take their medication(s), on a regular or intermittent basis. And it can notify the right people if a dosage is missed.

- Through the use of the included wireless pendant, OnKöl serves as an emergency response tool to notify family members if immediate attention is required.

- OnKöl can connect wirelessly via Bluetooth or by USB cable to virtually hundreds of medical devices from all manufacturers. That includes everything from blood pressure cuffs, glucose metres, heart-rate monitors, scales and many more. In each case, OnKöl collects the data, communicates it to the right people and stores the data for later use.

Source -http://www.onkol.net/

What are different data sources for Organizations?

Data generated by individuals are directly or indirectly consumed by different organisations. Different organisations have different sources of data generation. They mainly fall under one of the following categories.

- Directly from customers
- External data sources
- Internal data sources

Directly from customers:

Customer data can be captured in various modes either directly from customer transactions or through machine generated (IoT) devices/sensors.

- **Transaction Data :** As the name suggests, transactional data is information gathered via online and offline transactions during different points of sale. The data includes vital details like transaction time, location, products purchased, product prices, payment methods, discounts/coupons used, and other relevant quantifiable information related to transactions.

- **Machine/ Application Logs :**Machine logs are generated by appliances, applications, machinery, and networking equipment, (switches, routers, firewalls, etc). Every event, along with its information, is sequentially written to a log file containing all of the logs. Machine logs information indirectly captured while customer activities. This information is useful for tracking customer footprints and understanding customer engagement with applications.

- **Interaction with Customers:** Direct interaction with customers either on phone call, video call or any survey could help generate related data for the organisation. It is a feedback mechanism to improve services or to validate customer satisfaction level.

Internal Data Source

Internal sources of data reflect those data that are under the control of the organisation. Most of the time Internal data combines with external data to get more significant insight. Internal data is more unique to business and adds more values.

Once you identify which data you need, it's good practice to first consider which information is already available within the organisation. Sometimes data is already available within the company but it is forgotten or not aware of, especially in bigger organisations it is obvious that data is spreaded across multiple divisions.

Even if data is not available within an organisation, it's important to evaluate whether a company has capability to generate that data using new systems, products, customers, employees etc from outside.

Some example of internal data are:

There are a number of impactful, internal places that companies can look to mine data. These include:

Transactional Data: One of the powerful sources of data residing within a company is its financial and transactionals data. You can mine both current and historical data to get more business insight. Transactional data provides customer detail information like customers shopping trends, customers activities and behaviours information.

Customer Relationship Management System: Keeps customers key information like company's location, regions, and more about customers needs and communication information. It also keeps sales details and potential customers lead details.

Internal Documents: Internal documentation and content management is more important than ever before. Digital copy of internal documentation can provide a robust source of information. It also helps to define business and data glossaries.

Master Data: The information that is shared across organisations as enterprise data to analyse and drive business processes for operational efficiency.

External Data Source

Internal data is unique and limited to your business , it's just a snapshot of what's happening within your business however external data can provide you with global data. For example, job portals could provide you data about Job seekers. In the same way, there are many organisations who sell their data as a service. Big companies like Amazon, IBM, Microsoft etc provide niche data specialised in the industries. So, even if you are looking for some niche industry specific data, there is a high chance somebody has already collected that data and is readily available in the market.

Some free data available in the markets are:

- **Government Dataset**

  Many federal governments also provide several helpful informational sources that help today's enterprises get a better picture of the public.

  - **Data.gov**: This site was recently set up by federal authorities as part of the U.S. government's promise to make as much data as possible available. Best of all, these details are free, and accessible online. Here, companies will find a wealth of data, including information related to consumers, agriculture, education, manufacturing, public safety and much more.

  - **Data.gov.uk**: Businesses looking for a more global picture can look to this site, where the U.K. government has amassed an incredible amount of metadata dating back to 1950.

o   **Healthdata.gov**: Health care information can also be incredibly powerful for companies in that industry, as well as those operations in other sectors. This site provides more than 100 years of U.S. health care information, including datasets about medicare, population statistics and epidemiology.

Social media platform

- One of the most robust external data sources is social media channels, including Facebook, Instagram and Twitter. These sites have become incredibly popular – not only for individual customers, but for corporations as well. Social media data can be incredibly telling, offering insights into both positive and negative brand feedback, as well as trends, activity patterns and customer preferences. For instance, if a company notices that a large number of social media users are seeking a specific type of product, the business can move to corner the market and address these needs – all thanks to social media big data insights.

    Social media data that is useful to many companies, that will help to get answer the following questions:

    o   Who is my target audience?
    o   What social networks do they use regularly?
    o   How do they interact with social media networks?

Once you've answered these questions, it's much easier to narrow down the social media data and after looking at the behaviour and engagement data, the company determines their target audience. That will help to define marketing strategy

Dove – Connecting with their target audience

Dove's goal is to make women feel good about themselves. They know their target market and create content that tells a story that women can relate to. Dove did some research and found that 80 percent of women came across negative chatter on social media. Dove's goal was to change that and make social media a more positive experience. As a result, Dove teamed up with Twitter and built a tool to launch the #SpeakBeautiful Effect, that breaks down which body- related words people use the most and when negative chatter appears during the day.

According to Dove, women were inspired by their message.

- #SpeakBeautiful was used more than 168,000 times.
- Drove 800 million social media impressions of the campaign.

Dove knows their audience. Knowing your audience is the only way you will engage with them. The best way for this is creating personas. Knowing what life stage they are in, if they're employed, what their interests are etc. will certainly help you when creating content. Then think about linking your audience to your brand values in order to create something just as successful as dove's campaign.

- **Google Trend**
  - Google Trends is one of the best sources here, providing statistical information on search volumes for nearly any term – and these datasets stretch back to nearly the dawn of the internet.

- **External reference data**
  Reference data is data that's used for categorising master data or relating to information outside business, like customer segments, business processes, countries, and zip codes. Reference data is a non-volatile and slow moving subset of master data.

Basic Information Principles

While any company capturing customer data for business purposes should follow the information principles.

If information is not captured or translated correctly it would be a loss of opportunities for any organisation or individuals.

Information is value assets:

- This principle is the foundation for any what follows and highlights the need for information to be valued in the same way as these other types of asset. It is important to note that the full value of information lies not just in its original purpose but in its potential to be reused for other purposes.

Information is managed

- Information should be managed – stored, protected and exploited according to its value.

- Information needs to consider the whole lifecycle of the information management, from identification of need, information acquisition, quality validation, control, protection, analysis and ultimately to archiving or destruction once the information has ceased to be useful.

- Information should follow integrity, availability, consistency principles.

- It is important that personal data is adequately protected.

- The organisational culture must support best practice in information management, and make sure everyone responsible for processing these business assets is professionally qualified and appropriately skilled. This principle therefore also includes the processes, roles, responsibilities, training, and organisational structure and culture needed to ensure the effective and efficient use of information.

Information is fit for purpose

- Information must be good quality and fit for business use and potential analysis purposes.

- The quality of information should also be regularly monitored to ensure that they at least meet the levels that have been assessed as necessary.

- Quality includes factors such as accuracy, validity, reliability, timeliness, relevance and completeness.

- This principle doesn't require information to be perfect, only that it is the right quality for its intended use and that its quality characteristics are pragmatic, appropriate and transparent

Information is standardised and linkable

- Standardisation is important for structured information such as dataset definitions, and unstructured information such as Meta and reference data applied to documents.

- Standardisation within an organisation is important for staff to fully exploit the information; if an organisation uses widely accepted open standards it will unlock even more value.

- Standardisation is important both for the way information is recorded and in the way concepts are defined:

    - Format, eg date always being entered as dd-mm-yyyy.

    - Content, eg forename, surname, address, etc.

- o   Concepts, eg defining roles such as student, course, module, certificate, etc

- Even further value can be unlocked if information can be linked. A good example is document references and citations that allow the reader to draw on a wealth of associated information (this is the basis of the 'world wide web'). A similar concept can be applied to structured data, based on an understanding of the relationships between items and the use of consistent identifiers to reference authoritative sources (the basis of the 'semantic web'). For example, tagging funding information with an authoritative code for the organisation involved would allow it to be unambiguously linked with details of the organisation itself and third-party information about that organisation.

Information is accessible

- Individuals and organisations must be able to access information about themselves, along with an explanation of how that information is used by others. This may be either on request or, preferably, by making it available by default. In effect, such information should be considered as belonging to the individual, although entrusted to the care of a public body.

- This principle goes beyond minimum legal requirements. It advocates a proactive approach which makes it easy for individuals to access information about themselves, without having to make a request and even when access is not mandated in legislation. This might be achieved, for example, by making it securely available online. Information owners need to consider how this can work in practice, to enable users to view information and perform transactions, for example correcting inaccuracies.

- Clearly the desire to publish information does need to be balanced against constraints which may prevent this. Exclusions would include, for example, legally privileged information, information that is required to maintain security and information that is competitively sensitive.

Shared sector information is published

- This principle goes beyond adhering to minimum legal / regulatory requirements and advocates a proactive approach to presenting, formatting and promoting information in useful formats for wider consumption, without it needing to be specifically requested or mandated in legislation. [This principle is in line with the HEDIIP new landscape/shared sector language.]

- Consider the different channels available to publish information to the public. This includes internal publication processes, the use of publication hubs and relationships with third-party 'information intermediaries' such as commercial/ academic publishers.

- The benefits of publishing information should be balanced against possible risks and sensitivities, such as information which could compromise individuals' privacy, commercial and legally privileged information, and information that is required to maintain security.

Your Data with your responsibility

The most important type of information to keep private is personally identifiable information (PII). PII is "Information that can be used to distinguish or trace an individual's identity, either alone or when combined with other personal or identifying information that is linked or linkable to a specific individual."

Some Sample PII information includes
- Name
- Address
- Personal Unique ID (SSN)
- Vehicle number
- Address
- Biometric information

You also need to worry about what you post (and what others post about you) on social media and other sharing sites because these things serve as clues to your true identity when combined with the PII in the previous list.

Prevent Identity Theft :Identity theft occurs when someone gains access to your personal information and pretends to be you online. Individuals who have accessed your personal data can retrieve your login information for various websites or commit cyber crimes such as tax fraud, all while posing as you. Identity theft is the type of crime that can have long-lasting repercussions for both your digital privacy and your online reputation.

- **Only fill out required fields**: When you must fill out a profile or online form to use a product or service, only fill out the fields that are absolutely necessary and offer as few details about yourself as possible.

- **Never Share your data :**If you receive an email from a company you do business with, don't click on any links or attachments. Doing so might download a virus that could scan your entire computer and transmit all your data back to criminals. Instead, contact the company the email is supposedly from to verify that it sent the email.

- **Wipe old devices** before you discard them: Someone could easily access valuable personal data about you on old computers, tablets, or phones.

- **Don't share your banking information with anyone**: It's very easy for someone to withdraw money from your account if they know your bank account and routing numbers.

- **Only make online purchases from secure sites:** Look for the "S" after the "http" in the website's address. This means that the site is protected by Secure Sockets Layer (SSL) encryption.

- **Never save your payment information online:** According to a study by CreditCards.com, roughly 100 million Americans store their credit or debit card information in an app or on a website to make future purchases more convenient. However, having your financial data on a website makes it easier for hackers to shop there too.

- **Use strong passwords:** A strong password should contain at least 12 characters; include numbers, symbols, and capital letters; not be a dictionary word; and not rely on obvious substitutions

- **Enable 2-factor authentication:** This added step of typing in a secret code that is sent to your email when you attempt to log in can help you protect all your accounts.

Your Data with Company responsibility

- **Focus on Critical Data** : Collecting unnecessary data leads to becoming overloaded and uncomfortable for customers. Make sure the company only collects data that are actually useful and critical.

- **Data Security is essential:** One of the most important parts of customer data management is data protection from unauthorised access, use, change, disclosure, and destruction. No matter what type of data you're collecting from your individual customers, they want to know that their information is safe.

- **Data Accuracy** : Data inaccuracy can also happen if data collection events or required policies aren't set up properly. For example, even a simple data point such as dates can cause data inaccuracy. Are you collecting dates in the MM/DD/YYYY format or are you using DD/MM/YYYY? Customer data has to be collected in an accurate and reliable way.

- **Comply with Data Regulation:** As data privacy becomes more important to the public, companies are going to see more governments enacting laws similar to the General Data Protection Regulation (GDPR) and the California Consumer Privacy Act (CCPA)

Summary

In this chapter, a brief introduction to different data sources for individuals and organisations is outlined. Discussion includes

- Human generated data is data generated through human activities, such as response to email, photo upload on social media or publishing articles etc. Human generated data can be intentionally or unknowingly.

- Machine generated data is through devices, with IoT evaluation, machive / device generated data is very crucial and huge.

- Internal data source: This data source that is under control of the organisation.

- External data source: this data source is readily available and consumed from external sources like, government agencies, social media platforms etc.

- We talked about basic principles of Information that includes:

    o   Information is value assets:

    o   Information is managed

    o   Information is fit for purpose

    o   Information is standardised and linkable

    o   Information is accessible

    o   Shared sector information is published

- We also touched on responsibilities to protect your data as an individual or as a company.

References

- https://www.aunalytics.com/understanding-analytics-part-2-top-external-sources-of-big-data/
- https://ostmarketing.com/5-outstanding-social-media-marketing-case-studies/
- https://www.gloucestershire.gov.uk/media/2091604/information-management-principles.pdf
- https://www.reputationdefender.com/blog/privacy/top-ten-reasons-keep-your-personal-information-private
- https://segment.com/resources/cdp/customer-data-management/

Three

Save your Data

It's amazing how much data is out there. The question is how do we put it in a form that's usable?

-Bill Ford Jr.

Introduction

So far we discussed the importance of data and its different ways to collect the data. In this chapter, we will discuss more on how collected data is stored. Data storage essentially means that files and documents are recorded digitally and saved in a storage system for future use. Data storage can occur on physical hard drives, disk drives, USB drives or virtually in the cloud.

Depending upon the format of data, data could store in different storage. For example, in Priya's life she explores different apps and data content throughout her day activities.

	Activities	Data Sources	Content format
	Priya checks her emails before walks	Human generated	Structured Data Structural
	Priya checks Weather before calling Anna	Human generated	Structured Data
	Priya uses Smart watch for morning walk	Device generated Data	Semi Structured
	Priya did Card payment on juice shop	Device generated	Structured Data
	Priya and Anna took selfie and post on social media	Human and device generated	Structural Data Unstructured Data
	Priya did shopping through Amazon sites	Human Generated	Structural Data

Content Format

Structured data is when data is in a standardised format, has a well-defined structure, complies to a data model, follows a persistent order, and is easily accessed by humans and programs. This data type is generally stored in a database.

Examples of structured data include dates, names, addresses, credit card numbers, etc.

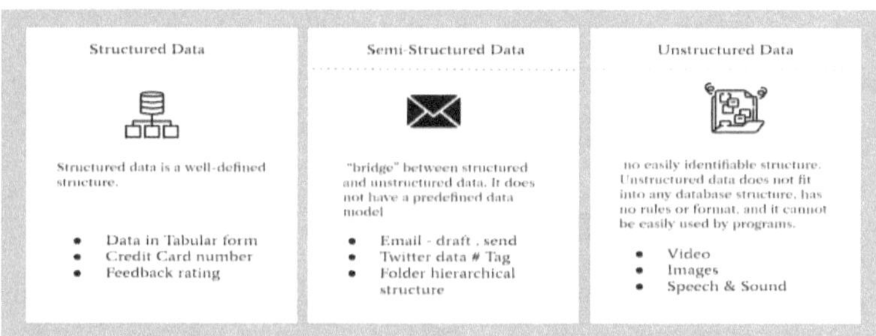

Unstructured data typically categorised as qualitative data, and does not conform to any other model and has no easily identifiable structure. There is no organisation to it and it cannot be stored in any logical way. Unstructured data does not fit into any database structure, has no rules or format, and it cannot be easily used by programs.

Semi Structured Data: Semi-structured data (e.g., JSON, CSV, XML) is the "bridge" between structured and unstructured data. It does not have a predefined data model and is more complex than structured data, yet easier to store than unstructured data.

Databases are everywhere and there are literally more than one million of them supporting various commercial and non-commercial activities. They range from file-based systems, through hierarchical, network, relational and object-oriented to NoSQL databases. Each of them fulfils a specific business goal and need. Hence, it may not always be straightforward to claim that one database type is better than the other.

Relational databases (RDB) have for many years governed the domain of data storage and management. Relational databases have spread worldwide across many businesses, and it is hard to find any company that is not using a relational database.

Recently, new needs have arisen requiring more data volume storage, better performance in form of higher retrieval frequency and processing, higher scalability and better support for agility. Unfortunately, relational databases cannot satisfy many of those needs. They are not well equipped for handling large complex sets of both structured and unstructured data in an efficient and cost-effective manner. For this reason, the database community is searching for solutions that better accommodate new business needs. Some of such solutions are NoSQL databases, the databases that promise to solve performance and scalability problems by storing and retrieving big data in non-tabular or semi-tabular forms.

How to choose right Data Storage for Data

Today's database market offers more than several hundreds of databases, all of them varying in data models, usage, performance, concurrency, scalability, security and the amount of supplier support provided. To stay competitive, many companies have to choose a database technology that is appropriate for their business operation.

Choosing a database is a different class of challenge. Let's understand different types of data we are generating and its nature.

 The ability to make a rigorous, informed choice of database technology requires a details knowledge of the following:

1. Deep understanding of the application problem at hand.
2. Knowledge of database semantics, including distributed computing fundamentals.
3. Skill in seeing through enterprise software marketing.

This isn't a set of talents easily found or obtained. Unfortunately, making a non-rigorous, uninformed choice of database technology can be a terminal mistake for an application.

Regardless of the type of database you're considering, the first critical step is defining your needs. For a minor purchase, this step might involve a quick conversation with other staff, but for a large, mission-critical piece of software, it might take months of work.

It starts with a question

- *What is a business application for?*
- *What nature of data are you looking to store?*
- *What data growth are you expecting?*
- *What if the database goes down and its implication?*

A database selection process is an initial part of an overall database lifecycle management process. This initial part proceeds with the installation of the selected database and adaptation of its hardware and software environments.

Evaluate Different Databases

Structured data is a well-defined structure, also known as quantitative data. It is typically managed using Structured Query Language (SQL), often in a relational database that allows users to quickly create and access structured data.

The benefit of structured data is its labelling to describe its attributes and relationships with other data. This data structure is easily searchable using a human or algorithmically generated query.

Only 20% of world-data are in structural form and 80% are either semi structured or unstructured data.

Biggest source of structural data comes from transaction information, customer information, product information and process details. However, large portions of data are non-quantifiable. Structural data are easily used in machine learning and artificial intelligence.

Relational Database

Data in the relational model is stored in tables and the tables consist of rows and columns. A row in a table describes a certain instance and an instance can be accessed by using identifiers known as primary keys. Tables implement relationships with themselves by storing foreign keys in the columns referring to the related tables. Information is retrieved by comparing the data value you wish to retrieve with search criteria written in a declarative programming language called Structured Query Language (SQL).

Relational databases can be two types

- OLTP (Row Oriented)
- OLAP (Column Oriented)

OLTP (Online Transactional Processing)

 OLTP, or online transactional processing, enables the real-time execution of large numbers of database transactions by large numbers of people, typically over the internet.

A database transaction is a change, insertion, deletion, or query of data in a database. OLTP systems (and the database transactions they enable) drive many of the financial transactions we make every day, including online banking and ATM transactions, e-commerce and in-store purchases, and hotel and airline bookings, to name a very few. In each of these cases, the database transaction also remains as a record of the corresponding financial transaction. OLTP can also drive non-financial database exchanges, including password changes and text messages.

In OLTP, the common, defining characteristic of any database transaction is its atomicity (or indivisibility)—a transaction either succeeds as a whole or fails (or is cancelled). It cannot remain in a pending or intermediate state.

Main Characteristic of OLTP application

- **Small Transactions:**OLTP systems typically read and manipulate highly selective, small amounts of data; the data processing is mostly simple and complex joins are relatively rare. There is always a mix of queries and DML workload. For example, one of many call centre employees retrieves customer details for every call and enters customer complaints while reviewing past communications with the customer.

- **Enable multi-user access to the same data, while ensuring data integrity**: OLTP systems rely on concurrency algorithms to ensure that no two users can change the same data at the same time and that all transactions are carried out in the proper order. This prevents people from using online reservation systems from double-booking the same room and protects holders of jointly held bank accounts from accidental overdrafts.

- **High Concurrency**: Due to the large user population, the short response times, and small transactions, the concurrency in OLTP environments is very high. A requirement for thousands of concurrent users is not uncommon.

- **High Availability**: The availability requirements for OLTP systems are often extremely high. An unavailable OLTP system can impact a very large user population, and organisations can suffer major losses if OLTP systems are unavailable. For example, a stock exchange system has extremely high availability requirements during trading hours.

Business use cases

- ATM machines (this is the classic, most often-cited example) and online banking applications
- Credit card payment processing (both online and in-store)
- Order entry (retail and back-office)
- Online bookings (ticketing, reservation systems, etc.)

- Record keeping (including health records, inventory control, production scheduling, claims processing, customer service ticketing, and many other applications)

OLAP (for online analytical processing)

is software for performing multidimensional analysis at high speeds on large volumes of data from a data warehouse, data mart, or some other unified, centralised data store. It is a technology that enables analysts to extract and view business data from different points of view. Analysts frequently need to group, aggregate and join data. These OLAP operations in data mining are resource intensive. With OLAP data can be pre-calculated and pre-aggregated, making analysis faster.

Most business data have multiple dimensions—multiple categories into which the data are broken down for presentation, tracking, or analysis. For example, sales figures might have several dimensions related to location (region, country, state/province, store), time (year, month, week, day), product (clothing, men/women/children, brand, type), and more.

- **OLAP Cube:**The core of most OLAP systems, the OLAP cube is an array-based multidimensional database that makes it possible to process and analyse multiple data dimensions much more quickly and efficiently than a traditional relational database.

OLTP vs. OLAP

OLTP is optimised for executing online database transactions. OLTP systems are designed for use by frontline workers (e.g., cashiers, bank tellers, part desk clerks) or for customer self-service applications (e.g., online banking, e-commerce, travel reservations).

OLAP, on the other hand, is optimised for conducting complex data analysis. OLAP systems are designed for use by data scientists, business analysts, and knowledge workers, and they support business intelligence (BI), data mining, and other decision support applications.

- OLTP systems use a relational database that can accommodate a large number of concurrent users and frequent queries and updates, while supporting very fast response times. OLAP systems use a multidimensional database—a special kind of database created from multiple relational databases that enables complex queries involving multiple data facts from current and historical data. (An OLAP database may be organised as a data warehouse.)

Relational Database options includes

- Oracle
- MySQL
- PostgreSQL
- IBM-DB2
- MariaDB
- Microsoft SQL Server

NoSQL Database

Nosql/Not Only SQL is a type of database that is used for storing a wide range of data sets. It is not a relational database as it stores data not only in tabular form but in several different ways. Since this non-relational database design does not require a schema, it offers rapid scalability to manage large and typically unstructured data sets. It came into existence when the demand for building modern applications increased. Thus, NoSQL presented a wide variety of database technologies in response to the demands.

 NoSQL is also type of distributed database, which means that information is copied and stored on various servers, which can be remote or local. This ensures availability and reliability of data. If some of the data goes offline, the rest of the database can continue to run.

Today, companies need to manage large data volumes at high speeds with the ability to scale up quickly to run modern web applications in nearly every industry. In this era of growth within cloud, big data, and mobile and web applications, NoSQL databases provide that speed and scalability, making it a popular choice for their performance and ease of use.

NOSQL database supports Structured, Semi- Structured and Unstructured databases.

Key Value

A key-value store consists of a set of key-value pairs with unique keys. The key is used as an identifier for searches and the value store includes the aggregate. In the industry, key-value databases are used for managing less complex data. Due to this simple structure, it only supports get and put operations.

Key	Values
User2:Friends	{23,76,120,89}
User2:Setting	{Theme:dark,cook
User3:Friends	{ 34,1,45,67,89}

Popular Databases
- Memcached,
- Redis
- DynamoDB

Popular Use Cases
- User preference and profile stores
- Product recommendations based on browsing data
- Shopping carts

Document Store

As suggested by the name, document databases store data as documents. They can be helpful in managing semi-structured data, and data are typically stored in JSON, XML, or BSON formats. This keeps the data together when it is used in applications, reducing the amount of translation needed to use the data. Developers also gain more flexibility since data schemas do not need to match across documents (e.g. name vs. first_name). However, this can be problematic for complex transactions, leading to data corruption. Popular use cases of document databases include content management systems and user profiles. An example of a document-oriented database is MongoDB, the database component of the MEAN stack.

```
{
Order_id : 123,
Customer: {Name:Priya, Age:27},
Product: Mobile:Iphone, Accessories:Charger},
Total Cost: 2345


}
```

Popular offerings include
- CouchDB
- RethinkDB
- MongoDB

Business use cases
- Mobile apps that require fast iterations
- Event logging, online shopping, content management and in-depth analytical processing
- Retail catalogues with product attributes

Wide-column store

These databases store information in columns, enabling users to access only the specific columns they need without allocating additional memory on irrelevant data. This database tries to solve for the shortcomings of key-value and document stores, but since it can be a more complex system to manage, it is not recommended for use for newer teams and projects. Apache HBase and Apache Cassandra are examples of open-source, wide-column databases.

Apache HBase is built on top of Hadoop Distributed Files System that provides a way of storing sparse data sets, which is commonly used in many big data applications. Apache Cassandra, on the other hand, has been designed to manage large amounts of data across multiple servers and clustering that spans multiple data centres. It's been used for a variety of use cases, such as social networking websites and real-time data analytics.

Row A	Column 1	Column 2	Column 3
	Value	Value	Value
Row B	Column 1	Column 2	Column 3
	Value	Value	Value

Popular offerings include
- Cassandra
- Google BigTable
- HBase

Business use cases

- Security and stock market analytics
- Click stream analytics
- IoT and telemetry

Graph store

This type of database typically houses data from a knowledge graph. Data elements are stored as nodes, edges and properties. Any object, place, or person can be a node. An edge defines the relationship between the nodes. For example, a node could be a client, like IBM, and an agency like Ogilvy. An edge would be to categorise the relationship as a customer relationship between IBM and Ogilvy.

Graph databases are used for storing and managing a network of connections between elements within the graph. Neo4j, a graph-based database service based on Java with an open-source community edition where users can purchase licence for online backup and high availability extensions, or pre-package licensed version with backup and extensions included.

Data model: G = (V, E): Graph-Property Modell
Interface: Traversal algorithms, queries, transactions.

Popular offerings include

- Neo4j
- InfiniteGraph
- OrientDB

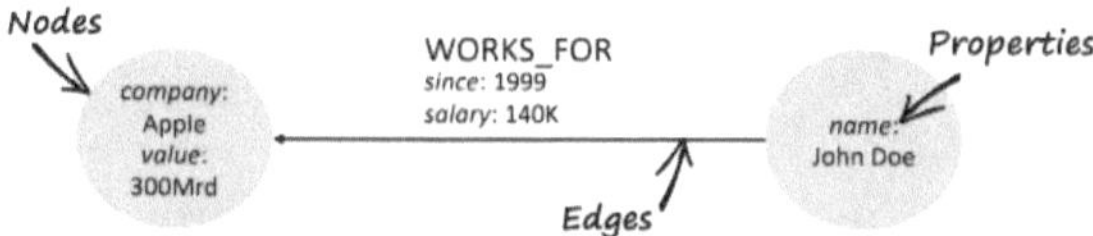

Business use cases

- Fraud detection
- Real-time recommendation engines
- Master data management
- Network and IT operations
- Identity and access management

In Memory In-memory databases are purpose-built databases that rely primarily on memory for data storage, in contrast to databases that store data on disk or SSDs. In-memory data stores are designed to enable minimal response times by eliminating the need to access disks.

In-memory databases are ideal for applications that require microsecond response times or have large spikes in traffic such as gaming leaderboards, session stores, and real-time analytics.

Popular offerings include

- SAP HANA
- Memcached
- Apache Ignite

Business use cases

- Real-time banking, retail, advertising, medical device analytics, machine learning.
- Online interactive gaming
- Processing of streaming sensor data
- Applications in transport systems, network switches and routers
- Developing embedded software systems

Time Series

A time series database is designed especially for handling time series data or time-stamped data. Time series data can be collected from a range of events or metrics, but it is always across server periods of time rather than individual events. You can use time series data for monitoring, aggregating, downsampling, and tracking behaviours across time. A TSDB can be used for a variety of data and purposes, including monitoring application performance, storing server metrics and network data, analysing sensor data, tracking events, market trades, clicks, and more.

Popular offerings include

- InFluxDB
- Graphite
- Kdb+
- QuestDB

Business use cases

- Asset Management system - where assets tracking is crucial
- Autonomous trading algorithms continuously collect data on how the markets are changing to optimise returns, both in the short and long-term.
- Specially in IoT applications where processing of streaming sensor data and fetch data based on specific timeframe.

Geo Special	Geospatial data is information that describes objects, events or other features with a location on or near the surface of the earth. Geospatial data typically combines location information (usually coordinates on the earth) and attribute information (the characteristics of the object, event or phenomena concerned) with temporal information (the time or life span at which the location and attributes exist).

A geospatial database is optimised for storing and querying data that represents objects defined in a geometric space, such as vector data and raster data. With data volume growing exponentially, a geospatial database provides the best manageability and security to analyse large, complex, heterogeneous spatial data.

There are two primary forms of geospatial data: vector data and raster data.

Vector data is data in which points, lines and polygons represent features such as properties, cities, roads, mountains and bodies of water. For example, a visual representation using vector data might include houses represented by points, roads represented by lines and entire towns represented by polygons.

Raster data is pixelated or gridded cells which are identified according to row and column. Raster data creates imagery that's substantially more complex, such as photographs and satellite images.

Examples of geospatial data include:

- Vectors and attributes: Descriptive information about a location such as points, lines and polygons.
- Point clouds: A collection of co-located charted points that can be re-contextured as 3D models.
- Raster and satellite imagery: High-resolution images of our world, taken from above.
- Census data: Released census data tied to specific geographic areas, for the study of community trends.
- Cell phone data: Calls routed by satellite, based on GPS location coordinates.
- Drawn images: CAD images of buildings or other structures, delivering geographic information as well as architectural data.
- Social media data: Social media posts that data scientists can study to identify emerging trends.

Block Storage	Unstructured data like images, video ,audio, pdf etc are generally stored in a Block storage like, S3, Cloud Storage etc.

Database-as-a-Service

DBaaS (Database as a service) is a cloud computing managed service offering model that enables users to set up, operate, manage and scale with some form of access to a database without the need for setting it up on physical hardware, installing software, or configuring it for performance, database management by themselves.

Cloud service providers provides database services in three categories

- RDBMS
- NoSQL
- DW

Popular DBMS offerings include:

Cloud Vendor	RDBMS	NoSQL	DW
Amazon	Amazon RDS Amazon Aurora	DynamoDB Elastic Cache	Redshift
Google	Google Cloud SQL Google Cloud Spanner	Cloud Big Table Google Spanner	Cloud BigQuery
Microsoft	SQL Azure	Azure Cosmos Table Storage DocumentDB	
IBM	IBM Pg	IBM Cloudant IBM DataStax	

Benefits of Database-as-a-Service

Agility:

Cloud DBaaS applications are agile in nature, so they adapt seamlessly to any upgrades according to business or technology advancements. DBaaS allows rapid provisioning of database resources to provide new computing resources and storage facilities in the minimum possible time. Together, this adds agility and flexibility to development teams, no matter their size or industry.

Safeguard Your Data

Security is one of the most critical challenges in the DBaaS domain. As more and more enterprises host their data in the cloud, it's crucial for DBaaS providers to prevent unauthorised access to data resources, disallow misuse of data stored on third-party platforms, and ensure data confidentiality, integrity, and availability.DBaaS providers typically offer enterprise-level security that supports encryption and multiple layers of security to protect data at rest, in transit, and during processing.

Scale According to Business Needs

The DBaaS model provides automated and dynamic scaling. DBaaS providers adapt to workload changes and are able to manage load variations by increasing resources during peak hours without any service disruption, or by allocating fewer resources during periods of non-peak usage to help reduce costs. Users can quickly add storage and computing capacity to meet high processing demands while also defining usage threshold policies for how the system should behave during demand fluctuations.

High Availability

In today's fast-paced digital world, maintaining 24×7 operational uptime is a must for any modern business. Outages are directly proportional to the loss of revenue. As digital transformation becomes more and more essential, it's increasingly important that your application service should remain up 24/7 without any downtime. If there's any kind of system failure, the system should be intelligent enough to recover from the loss in no time.

The DBaaS model provides maximum high availability and runs at peak performance. It provides zero or no-data loss tolerance and eliminates a single point of failure. In case of any kind of failure in a single database instance, the platform automatically reroutes traffic to a replica/standby instance and maintains uptime. The model is intelligent enough to accept the database connections and allow enterprise developers to perform database queries even in the case of a system failure.

Increase operational efficiency

Since DBaaS is a service, you can start small with one node at a time and scale bigger without disrupting the business. Organisations can scale as they grow which is far more cost-efficient; by adding one or more nodes at a time and then spinning down resources that are no longer needed, IT teams can prevent costly overages.

Content Type	Database		Cloud Agnostic	AWS	Azure	GCP
Structured	Relational	OLTP	Oracle SQL Server MySQL PostgreSQL IBM-DB2	RDS Aurora	Azure SQL Database	Cloud SQL, Cloud Spanner
	Columnar	OLAP	Snowflake Cassendra HBASE	Redshift	Azure Synapse	Big Query
Semi Structured	Dictionary	Key Value	MongoDB Redis Apache Ignite	DynamoDB	Cosmos DB	Big Table
		In-Memory	Redis Memcached Apache Ignite	Elasticache	Azure Cache for Redis	Memory-store
	JSON,XML	Document	MongoDB CouchDB Solr Rethink DB	Document DB	Cosmos DB	Firestore
	Time series	Time Series	InFluxDB Graphite Kdb+ QuestDB	Time Stream	Cosmos DB	Big Table Big Query
	Location & Geo entities	Geo Spatial	Solr MongoDB Post GSI	Keyspaces	Cosmos DB	Big Table Big Query
	Entity Relationship	Graph	Neo4J Infinite Graph Orient DB	Neptune	Cosmos DB	Big Table
Un Structured	Audio Video Text Image	BLOB	HDFS File System	S3	BLOB Storage	Cloud Storage

Summary

In this chapter, we discussed the importance of databases, and different types of databases. We covered a basic overview of relational databases and its different kinds of relational databases, including OLTP and OLAP databases types.

We also talk about different kinds of NoSQL databases, key-value, document store, wide-column store, graph databases, in-memory and time Series databases.

- Data represents three different content types.
    - Structured Data
    - Unstructured Data
    - Semi Structured Data

- Structured data keeps relational database
- Relational databases have predefined structure, OLTP and OLAP are two different kinds of relational databases.
- No-SQL is not only sql which supports relational, non relational both kinds of data. NoSQL has different kinds of databases such as
    - Key Value databases
    - Document databases
    - Graph databases
    - In-memory databases
    - XML,JSON
    - Time Series databases
- Block storage is for unstructured data databases which includes filebase storage, S3, cloud storage and BLOB storage.

Four

Transfer and Transform your data

When you actually go into the business world and you look at the data, half of the data is missing, some of it doesn't make any sense, but you still have to use it. You can't say, 'I quit.'

– Dr. Goutam Chakraborty, Oklahoma State University

Introduction

Operational Data is available in the database, now the question is what next ? One of the main intentions of collecting data is to get insight from it, but one dataset might not be enough to extract meaningful information. In modern architecture, specific apps or services are available in the market to serve specific purposes. E.g. Salesforce for managing sales lead, master data management for customer information, Payment information is handled by different applications etc.

Data silo is a major challenge for many organisations, data that's controlled by one department or business unit and isolated from the rest of an organisation.

In this chapter, we will discuss more on how a data pipeline can break data silos and integrate with a centralized database system.

What is a Data Pipeline?

To understand better, let's take an analogy from manufacturing automated pipelines.

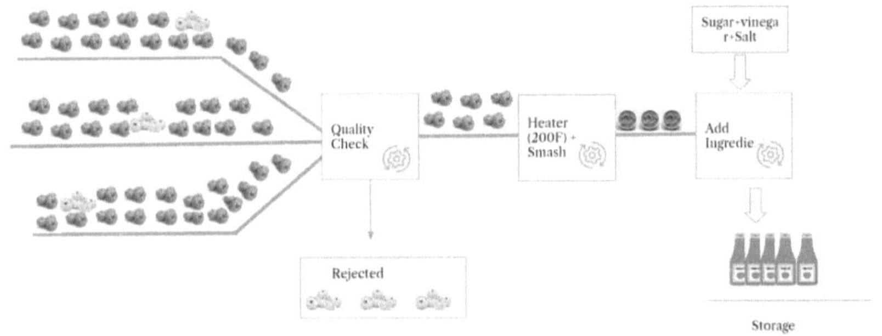

Journey from tomatoes to tomato ketchup includes multiple stages.

- Identify right sources of tomatoes

- Load tomatoes in a plant

- Verify the right quality of tomatoes, this process includes identifying damage.

- The tomato paste is typically manufactured using the "Hot Break" method. With this method, pulped tomatoes are heated to 200°F (90°C).

- Tomato ketchup is a condiment made by mixing concentrated tomato paste with water, sugar, vinegar, salt and seasonings.

- Store final ketchup into a bottle.

In the digital world, data pipeline also follows the same things, it goes through a single stage operation to multiple stages.

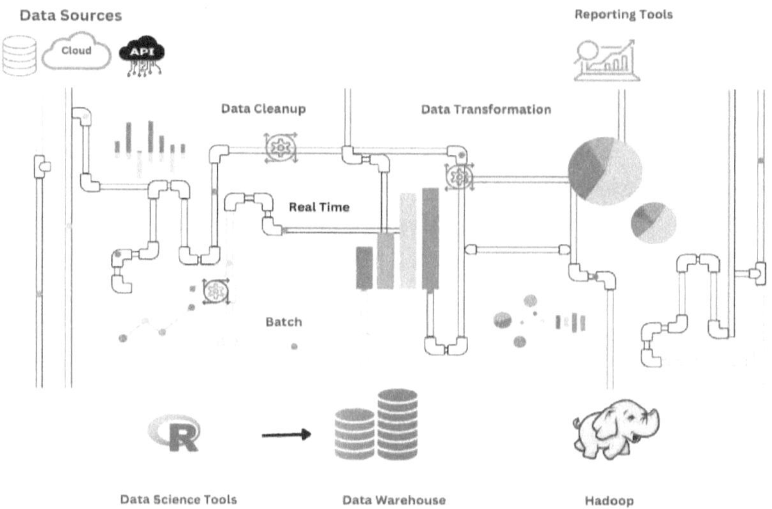

In other words, a data pipeline is a set of tools and processes used to automate the movement and transformation of data between a source system and a target repository.

While doing so, pipelines take care of extracting data from many disparate source systems, transforming and combining and, validating that data and finally loading into the target repository.

The complexity of a data pipeline depends on the size,state and structure of the source data. Simplest data pipeline includes dumping data from one source to another, e.g. extracting data from one source such as REST API and loading it to a destination such as a SQL table in a data warehouse.

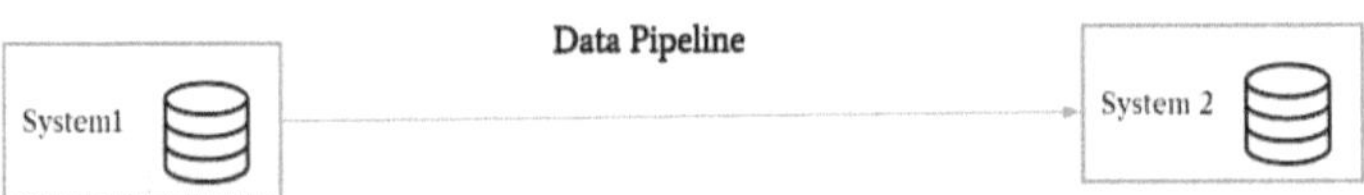

Types of Data Pipeline

There are two main types of data pipelines, which are batch processing and streaming data.

Batch Processing

As the name implies, batch processing loads "batches" of data into a repository during set time intervals, which are typically scheduled during off-peak business hours.Batch data pipelines are executed manually or recurrently. In each run, they extract all data from the data source, apply operations to the data, and publish the processed data to the data sink. They are done once all data has been processed.

Typical use cases for batch data pipelines have complex requirements on the data processing, such as joining dozens of different data sources (or tables), and are not time-sensitive. Examples include payroll, billing, or low-frequency reports based on historical data.

Batch Processing

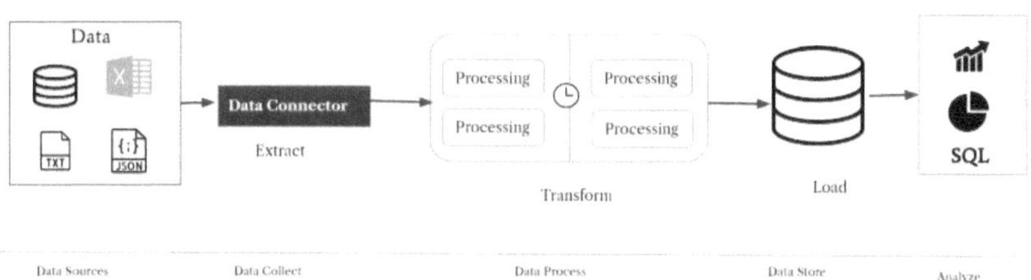

Batch processing generally supports non real time data transmission. This kind of data can take anywhere from hours to days to years to be created. In this scenario, the traditional ETL approach might be useful to extract the data, transform and clean it, and then load it into a target data store of choice.

ETL pipelines can support use cases that can rely on historical data, and are especially appropriate for small data sets which require complex transformations. Converting raw data to match the target system before it is loaded, allows for systematic and accurate data analysis in the target repository. ETL is an acronym for "Extract, Transform, and Load" and describes the three stages of this pipeline:

- ***Extract***: pulling raw data from a source (such as a database, an XML file or a cloud platform holding data for systems such as marketing tools, CRM systems, or transactional systems)

- ***Transform***: converting the format or structure of the dataset to match that of the target system

- ***Load***: placing the dataset into the target system which can be an application or a database, data lakehouse, data lake.

Extract Transform Load (ETL)

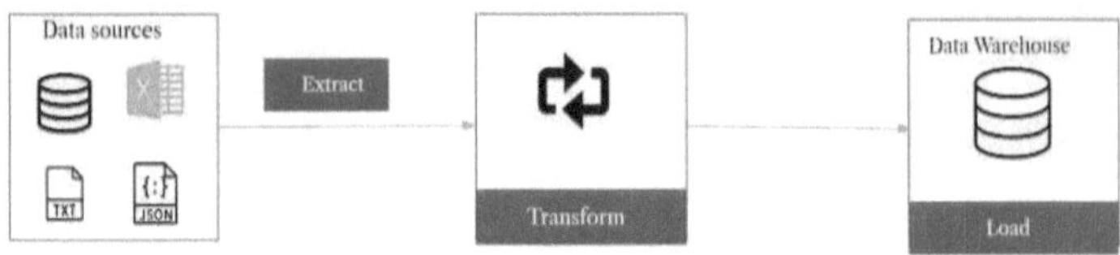

As of recently, ELT has become a lot more popular though. Compared to ETL, ELT allows an organisation to practically replicate the data over to their environment and then run whatever transformations they need on that raw data to capture valuable data insights.

Extract -Load -Transform (ELT)

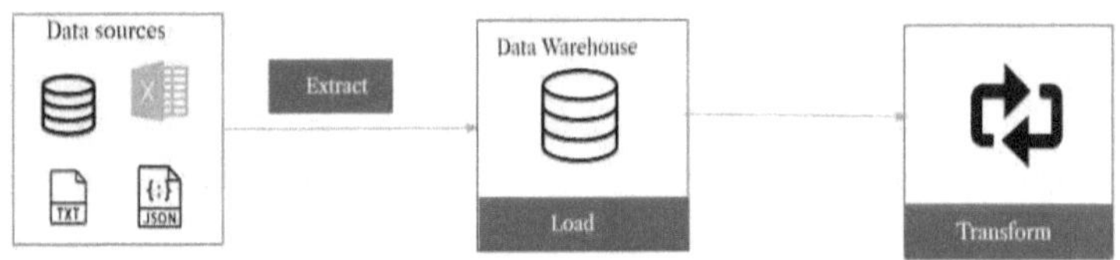

Streaming Data Pipelines

As opposed to batch data pipelines, streaming data pipelines are executed continuously, all the time. They consume streams of messages, apply operations, such as transformations, filters, aggregations, or joins to the messages, and publish the processed messages to another stream.

Stream processing is a low-latency way to capture information about events while they are in transit, processing the data. A data stream, or event stream, can include almost any type of information: social network or web browsing path data, factory production and other process data, stock or financial transaction details, patient data in a hospital, machine learning system data, IoT (Internet of Things).

For large, unstructured data sets and when timeliness is important, the ELT process is more appropriate ("Extract, Load, and Transform") than ETL.

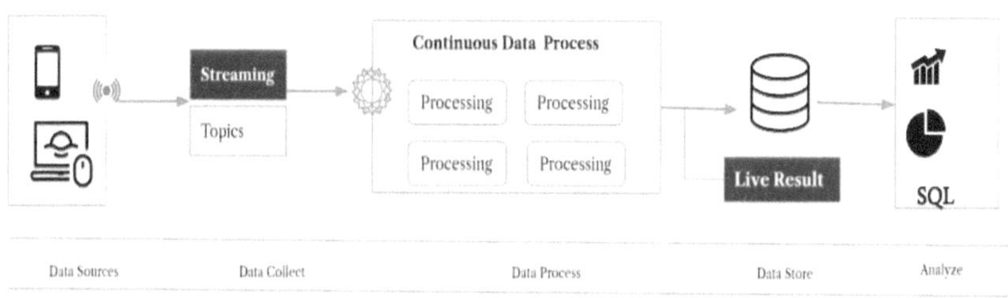

Streaming data pipelines keep data sinks always in sync with data sources. They minimise the gap between the time a change event occurs in the data source and the time the processed event arrives at the data sink.

Streaming/Batch Architecture

This architecture is called lambda architecture and is used when there is a need for both batch and streaming data. Although a lot of use cases can be handled by using one or the other, this gives us more flexibility when designing our overall architecture.

Real time data is data that comes in millisecond to second latency. To keep up with the data velocity, some ETL tools can't be leveraged and/or don't have the capabilities to keep up. Common real time streaming software's that are being leveraged today are Apache Kafka, Spark streaming and Amazon Kinesis etc.

Data Pipeline Components

So far we discussed data pipelines and types of data pipelines. In this section, we will discuss more about different components of data pipeline.

Data Pipeline Components

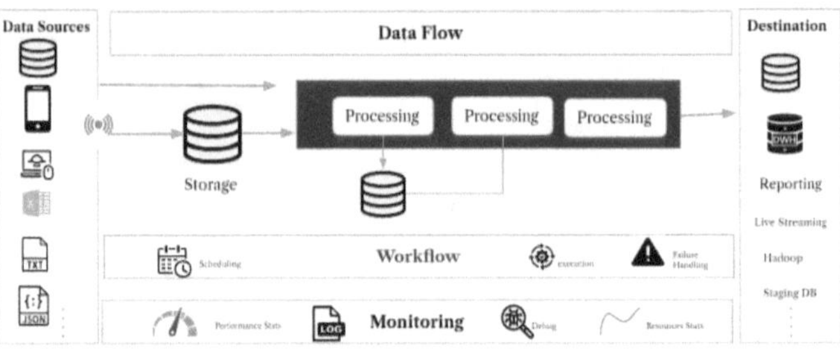

David Wells, a research analyst from Eckerson Group considers eight types of data pipeline components:

- Data Sources
- Destination
- Data Flow
- Storage
- Processing
- Workflow
- Monitoring

Origin: Origin is the initial point at which data enters into the pipeline. There could be multiple data sources like (IoT devices, application databases, social media data, public dataset etc). Data source could be the original transactional system or from any staging system.

Data Origin	
Direct from Sources	**From Storage**
<ul><li>Web and Social Media</li><li>Machine Generated Data</li><li>Human Generated</li><li>Transaction Data</li><li>Internal Data Source</li><li>External Data Sources</li></ul>	<ul><li>Staging</li><li>Data Warehouse</li><li>Data Mart</li><li>Operational Data Store</li><li>Master Data Store</li><li>Cloud Storage</li><li>Temporary Files</li></ul>

Destination: Destination also called a data sink, its final termination point to which data is delivered. Depending upon the use cases, destination could differ, it might be storage like data warehouse, data lake, or S3, any cloud storage.

How quick is data needed in the destination, decides the approach of the data pipeline, in some cases data needs to be real time, but in the same cases some delay would be fine.

Destination consumes or stores this pipeline data depending upon the business need. In some cases data pipeline data is directly reflected on the dashboard for reporting purposes rather than stored somewhere in the storage.

Commonly used data destination includes:

- Data warehouse: A data warehouse enables you to store, manage, and organise data. It usually has dashboards, analytics tools and reporting features to help you analyse and interpret your data.

- Data lake: A data lake is a system that allows you to store raw, unprocessed data at any scale

- Datamart: A data mart is a smaller, data storage option that usually focuses on one subset of data, like sales or leads.

Data Destination	
Storage	Application
<ul><li>Staging</li><li>Data Warehouse</li><li>Data Mart</li><li>Operational Data Store</li><li>Master Data Store</li><li>Cloud Storage</li></ul>	<ul><li>Reporting</li><li>Dashboard</li><li>BI</li><li>Analytics</li><li>Scorecards</li><li>Logging</li></ul>

Dataflow: The sequence of processes and data stores through which data moves to get from origin to destination.

A single data pipeline might contain multiple steps that help to ingest data into the pipeline, process the data and store the data. Entire orchestration is done by the dataflow.

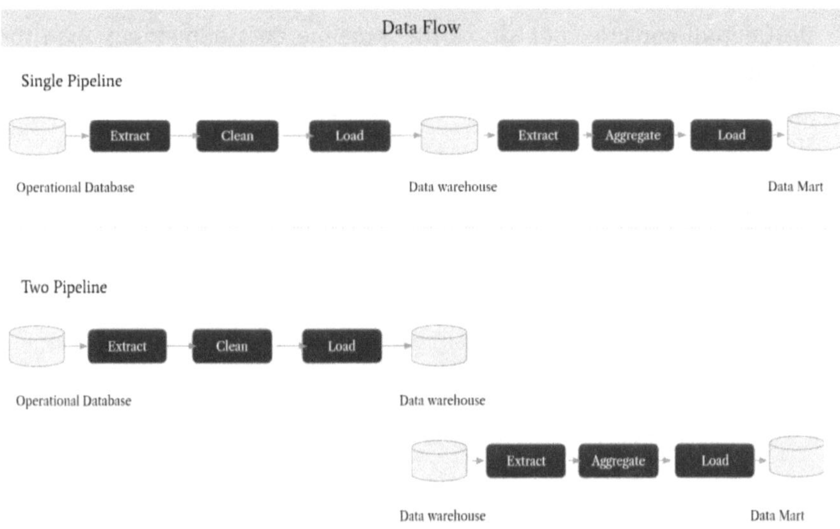

Storage: Storage refers to systems where data is preserved at different stages as it moves through the pipeline.

Data storage choices depend on various factors, for example, the volume of data, frequency and volume of queries to a storage system, uses of data, etc.

Data storage choices for data stores such as a data warehouse or data lake are architectural decisions that constrain pipeline design. Data storage choices for intermediate data stores are pipeline design decisions though standards, conventions, skills, and available technology are likely to limit the choices. In the last chapter, we covered detailing on data selection and technical evaluation process.

Processing. Processing includes activities and steps for ingesting data from sources, storing it, transforming it, and delivering it to a destination. While data processing is related to the dataflow, it focuses on how to implement this movement. For instance, one can ingest data by extracting it from source systems, copying it from one database to another one (database replication), or by streaming data.

Some common Data processes includes:

- **Data Ingestion** Is the process of obtaining and importing data in a data pipeline. Data ingestion is performed in many ways,including exporting data, data replication, data streaming or messaging etc. Depending upon business need options can be selected.

- **Data Transformation:** Is the process changing the format, structure, or values of data to meet specific needs or goals. Data transformation may be described as either "simple" or "complex", depending on the kinds of changes that must occur to the data before it is delivered to its target destination. Some common techniques used for data transformation include.

  - o **Standardisation** consistently encodes and formats data that is similar.

  - o **Conforming** ensures consistent meaning and content when the same data is stored in multiple files or databases.

  - o **Data cleansing** detects and corrects deficiencies in data quality.

  - o **Quality assurance** derives new data (metadata) that rates, scores, or otherwise describes the quality of data.

  - o **De-duplication** intelligently removes redundantly stored data.

  - o **Derivation** creates a new data value from one or more contributing data values using a formula or algorithm.

  - o **Appending** extends a dataset with additional attributes from another data source.

o **Aggregation** composes new data records by bringing together data from multiple records and applying formulas or algorithms. Aggregates may be either summaries or assemblies.

o **Sorting and sequencing** place data in the order that is best suited to the needs of analysis. Sorting prescribes the sequencing of records. Sequencing prescribes a sequence of fields within a record.

o **Pivoting** changes data orientation by swapping the positions of rows and columns.

o **Sampling** statistically selects a representative subset of a population of data.

o **Filtering** reduces a data set to contain only the data that is useful at the destination.

o **Masking** obscures data values for sensitive data.

o **Assembly and construction** build final format records in the form needed at a destination.

Workflow – Sequencing and dependency management of processes. A pipeline's workflow defines and manages the sequencing of its processes and their dependencies on each other. A workflow handles sequencing and dependencies at two levels–the level of individual tasks performing a specific function and the level of units, or jobs combining multiple tasks.

Open source tools like Airflow and Luigi structure the processes that make up the pipeline, automatically resolve dependencies, and give developers a way to visualise and organise data workflows.

Monitoring – Observing to ensure a healthy and efficient pipeline. Monitoring involves the observation of a data pipeline to ensure efficiency, reliability, and strong performance. Considerations in designing pipeline monitoring systems include what needs to be monitored, who will be monitoring it, what thresholds or limits are applicable, and what actions will be taken when these thresholds or limits are reached.

Tools and Technologies for Data Pipeline

There are many tools available in the market and the count is increasing day by day.

Some of common tools are highlighted below

Batch Data Pipeline Tools	• Informatica PowerCenter
	• IBM Info Sphere DataStage
	• Talend
	• Pentaho
	• Oracle Data Integrator
	• Panoply (ELT)
	Alteryx
Streaming Data Pipeline	• Apache Kafka
	• Apache Airflow
	• Apache Spark
	• Apache Storm
	• Stream Analytics
	• IBM Streams
	• SQK Stream
Cloud	• AWS Glue
	• Google Cloud Data Flow
	• Azure Data Factory

Implementation options for data pipelines

You can implement your data pipeline using cloud services by providers or build it on-premises.

On-premises data pipeline

To have an on-premises data pipeline, you buy and deploy hardware and software for your private data centre. You also have to maintain the data centre yourself, take care of data backup and recovery, do a health check of your data pipeline, and increase storage and computing capabilities. This approach is time- and resource-intensive but will give you full control over your data, which is a plus.

Cloud data pipeline

Cloud data infrastructure means you don't have physical hardware. Instead, you access a provider's storage space and computing power as a service over the internet and pay for the resources used. This brings us to a discussion of the pros of a cloud-based data pipeline.

- You don't manage infrastructure and worry about data security because it's the vendor's responsibility.
- Scaling storage volume up and down is a matter of a few clicks.
- You can adjust computational power to meet your needs.
- Downtime risks are close to zero.
- Cloud ensures faster time-to-market.

Disadvantages of cloud include the danger of a vendor lock: It will be costly to switch providers if one of the many pipeline solutions you use (i.e., a data lake) doesn't meet your needs or if you find a cheaper option. Also, you must pay a vendor to configure settings for cloud services unless you have a data engineer on your team.

How to design Pipelines Built ?

There are many factors to consider when designing data pipelines, and early decisions have tremendous implications for future success. The following section is meant to be a reference point for asking the right questions from the start of the data pipeline design process.

Numerous tools and services are available in the market and adding more with each day. Some are open source, some commercial and some are homegrown. Some are easy to implement with cloud services, some are complex, some written in Python, some in Java and other languages, and some with no code at all.

Building pipeline includes key tasks:

- ***Determine the Goal:*** When designing a data pipeline, the priority is to identify the outcome or value the data pipeline will bring to your company or product. At this stage, we ask relevant questions such as:

    o What are our objectives for this data pipeline?
    o How do we measure the success of the data pipeline?
    o What use cases will the data pipeline serve (reporting, analytics, machine learning)?
    o

- ***Identify Data Sources:*** Identify business values and map data entities to support business values. At this stage, it's critical to ask questions such as:

    o What are all the potential sources of data?
    o In what format will the data come in (flat files, JSON, XML)?
    o How will we connect to the data sources?

- ***Determine the data ingestion strategy*** : With the pipeline goal and data sources understood, we need to ask questions about how the pipeline will collect the data. At this point, we ask questions such as :
    o What communication layer will we be using to collect data (HTTP, MQTT, gRPC)?
    o Would we be utilising third-party integration tools to ingest the data?
    o Are we going to be using intermediate data stores to store data as it flows to the destination?
    o Are we collecting data from the origin in predefined batches or in real time?

- ***Design Data Processing Plan:***Once data has been ingested, it has to be processed and transformed for it to be valuable to downstream systems. At this stage, it's necessary to ask questions such as:

- o What data processing strategies are we utilising on the data (ETL, ELT, cleaning, formatting)?
  - o Are we going to be enriching the data with specific attributes?
  - o Are we using all the data or just a subset?
  - o How do we remove redundant data?

- **Setup Storage for output of the pipeline**: Once the data has been processed, we must determine the final storage destination for our data to serve various business use cases. At this step, we ask questions such as:

  - o Are we going to be using big data stores like data warehouses or data lakes?
  - o Would the data be stored on cloud or on-premises?'
  - o Which of the data stores will serve our top use cases?
  - o In what format will the final data be stored?

- **Plan the data workflow:** We then need to design the sequencing of processes in the data pipeline. At this stage, we ask questions such as:

  - o What downstream jobs are dependent on the completion of an upstream job?
  - o Are there jobs that can run in parallel?
  - o How do we handle failed jobs?

- **Implement a data monitoring and governance framework:** In this step, we establish a data monitoring and governance framework, which helps us observe the data pipeline to ensure a healthy and efficient channel that's reliable, secure, and performs as required. In this step, we determine:

  - o What needs to be monitored?
  - o How do we ensure data security?
  - o How do we mitigate data attacks?
  - o Is the data intake meeting the estimated thresholds?
  - o Who is in charge of data monitoring?

- ***Plan the data consumption layer:*** This final step determines the various services that'll consume the processed data from our data pipeline. At the data consumption layer, we ask questions such as:

  - What's the best way to harness and utilise our data?
  - Do we have all the data we need for our intended use case?
  - How do our consumption tools connect to our data stores?

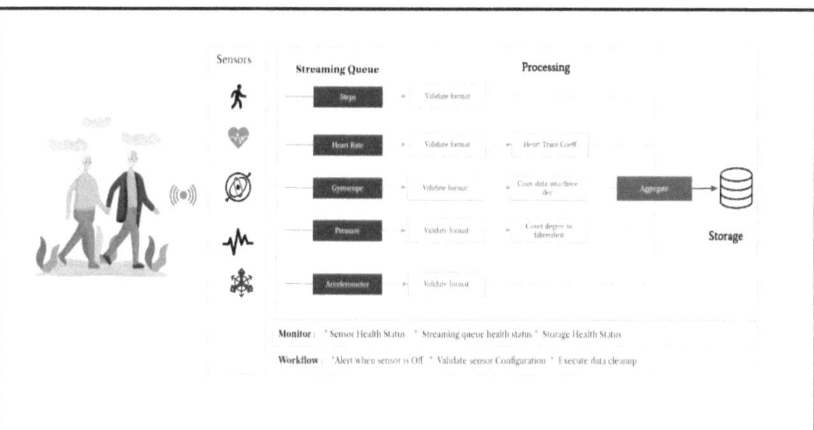

Let's take an example where our real time data passes through this pipeline.

Smartwatches are convenient to wear and have the capability to collect data in a continuous manner given that the battery is charged periodically. Furthermore, they provide additional benefits to the participant including managing their calendar, text messaging and making phone calls which can have a significant impact on their acceptance and wear time. The major contribution for smartwatches adoption is its health monitoring sensors. The concomitant collection of location information via GPS to understand community mobility patterns, physical activity data from an accelerometer and reported health symptoms or events is ideal for creating a narrative of personal health information in a remote and interactive manner.

Smartwatches collects sensor data (e.g., accelerometer, gyroscope, location, and heart rate) at specified and customizable frequencies and sends them to the server.

Data is uploaded to the server over a WiFi or 4G network connection. The use of WiFi connection or cellular data for data transmission allows for having the collected data available on the server in real-time and in a minimally intrusive manner.

Beside sending its collected data, the application requests the server to receive configuration parameters and adjusts its sensor utilisation, accordingly.

Domain	Description	Collection Methods
Mobility and Activity	**Physical activity**: the average minutes per day spent Total activity, light, moderate & vigorous activity, sedentary	Accelerometer trigger and GPS longitude and latitude
	Walk speed: GPS is triggered during a two-min bout of continuous of activity until the end of the bout (1 min of no activity detection) GSP data processed using previously validated Personal Activity and Location Measurement	

The smartwatch application can serve as a reporting tool to obtain participants' reports of their health.

There are two components in the Smart watches

- Smart watch collecting sensor data and keep within a small memory storage
- Servers collect data from sensors and validate and transform data using different processing mechanisms.

Data Sources: Multiple sensors generate and capture activities data e.g. GPS collect longitude and latitude data, Heart rate sensors collect frequency data.

Data Collector: Each sensor passes data to a real time streaming queue like Kafka, Apache Spark etc. Separate queue for each sensor data.

Data Cleaning and Aggregation: The next step after raw data collection is the data cleaning, e.g. time variables are usually calculated for longer epochs; converting datetime to epochs or vice versa.

Mostly sensor data collected in JSON format. If the format is not correct then it rejects the payload. Once payload is validated then it transforms data to business format, e.g. Heart Rate supposed to be 10Hz, convert temperature degree to fahrenheit.

Aggregate all sensors data into one common Json

```
{

    Steps : OFF
    Coordinates: OFF
    Accelerometer:0.32.4.46.7.93
    Gyroscope: -1.2.0.30.0.91
    Heart Rate: 85
    UV Index: OFF
    Battery : 100
    Time:1665656530
    DeviceId:135454

}
```

Data Storage: The collected data are validated and processed in the previous steps (by the smartwatch application and the Application Manager) before reaching the Data Storage module. This module performs the final checks and modifications and stores data in a high-performance database.The data inserted into the database include an entry for each data item transferred from the watch as well as metadata specifying a timestamp of when the transfer was processed, as well as the size of the received data.

Visualisation

Web-based user interface that presents summary statistics of the collected data (e.g., duration of data collection, size of the accumulated data) and the status of the watches (e.g. collecting/stopped, battery level). The web portal is also capable of visualising the calculated variables from the data, which is an effective way to reduce errors during data collection phase.

Summary

- A data pipeline is a set of tools and processes used to automate the movement and transformation of data between a source system and a target repository.

- Data Pipeline consolidates data from all your disparate sources into one common destination, enabling quick data analysis for business insights. They also ensure consistent data quality, which is absolutely crucial for reliable business insights.

- For building an effective pipeline you need to evaluate key tasks including , Identify business goals , data sources, data processing steps and destination.

- David Wells, a research analyst from Eckerson Group considers eight types of data pipeline components. Data Origin, Data Destination, Data Flow, Storage, Processing, Workflow, Monitoring and Technology.

- Data Pipelines are two types 1) Batch Data processing 2) Stream data processing

- ETL / ELT are two way data processes depending upon the business needs.

- Data pipeline can be implemented in On premises data pipeline and cloud native data pipeline.

References

- https://www.qlik.com/us/data-integration/data-pipeline
- https://www.altexsoft.com/blog/data-pipeline-components-and-types/
- https://www.simplilearn.com/what-is-data-pipelining-article
- https://www.striim.com/blog/guide-to-data-pipelines/
- https://datacater.io/blog/2020-08-11/batch-vs-streaming.html
- https://dingyuliang.me/big-data-pipeline-open-source-technologies/
- https://www.stitchdata.com/resources/analytic-vs-transactional-database/
- https://databand.ai/blog/building-data-pipelines/

Five

Explore your data- Mining

"The data is often sitting there and waiting to be used, but business leaders simply aren't asking the right questions that help us to structure it in such a way that we can deliver answers."

Introduction

Data is sitting ideal in storage and waiting to be used. Business leader needs to ask the right questions so that data can be structured in a way that it can deliver answers. There is so much data in organisations that it is hard to know where to start. A lot of organisations are still struggling to understand how their data support value creation. There is no magic wand available which transforms raw data into actionable data overnight. Choosing the right data and right techniques is challenging itself. This is why starting with a use case or a real commercial problem that needs solving with data can be the most fruitful approach.

"There is a strong desire to boost competitive insight and efficiency using analytics, but it is not being fed into core business strategies: a missed opportunity," says Laurie Miles, director of analytics at SAS UK and Ireland.

"With AI now top of mind for many, it's more important than ever to have a powerful, streamlined analytics capability."

In this chapter, we will cover how you can make your data into actionable data with different techniques and available tools.

In this chapter, we will cover data mining techniques. Data mining is the process of extracting meaningful information from data. Data mining process includes tools and techniques that use statistical, mathematical and analytical capability to find patterns and insights from the data.

Let's go inside data mining.

What is Data Mining?

Data mining is a procedure to extract information from a huge set of data, also known as mining knowledge from data. Data mining can be done mostly on relational databases like data warehouse, transaction data or RDBMS databases.

Data Mining techniques are at the forefront in the process of discovery. Data mining has opened a world of possibilities for business. This field of computational statistics compares millions of isolated pieces of data and is used by companies to detect and predict consumer behaviour. Data mining, also known as knowledge discovery in data (KDD), is the process of uncovering patterns and other valuable information from large data sets. Given the evolution of data warehousing technology and the growth of big data, adoption of data mining techniques has rapidly accelerated over the last couple of decades, assisting companies by transforming their raw data into useful knowledge.

Main intention for data mining is to search patterns and trends with given data.

Business enterprises are beginning to realise that customers' information like buying patterns, behaviours trends are the most valuable information. Competitiveness increasingly depends on the quality of decision making and learning to make quality decisions from the past transactions and decisions. Organisations can get immense benefit in the area of marketing, sales and product innovations if customers' buying patterns, their wants and needs are discovered from the large volume of data.

The data mining techniques that underpin these analyses can be divided into two main purposes; they can either describe the target dataset or they can predict outcomes through the use of machine learning algorithms.

Some examples where data mining utilised are:

Marketing: Data mining is used to explore new customer segments and identify opportunities. By analysing the relationships between different parameters such as customer age, gender, location etc, companies can guess customer behaviours or possible prospects. Companies define their marketing strategy based on the available data and its patterns.

Retailer: Data Mining helps the supermarket and retail sector owners to know the choices of the customers. Looking at the purchase history of the customers, the data mining tools show the buying preferences of the customers.

Market basket analysis is data mining technique used by retailers to increase sales by better understanding customer purchase patterns. It involves analysing large data sets, such as purchase history, to reveal product groupings, as well as products that are likely to be purchased together.

With the help of these results, the supermarkets design the placements of products on shelves and bring out offers on items such as coupons on matching products, and special discounts on some products.

Telecom Service : Data mining helps to identify customer usage patterns including calling patterns or data usage patterns, these patterns helps telecom services to decide the best recharge plan for prepaid and postpaid services. Also helps to identify subscribers who could potentially move from prepaid to postpaid payment methods.

Banking: Banking uses data mining to better understand market risks. It is commonly used in credit rating, fraud detection, purchasing patterns and marketing campaigns. Data mining allows banks to minimise risk and manage regulatory compliance obligations.

Medicine: Data mining enables more accurate diagnostics. With historical patient's information such as medical records, physical examinations and treatment patterns allow medical researchers to find patterns and correlations between lines of treatment and diseases. Data mining enables medical research to be more effective, efficient and cost effective.

Crime Prevention

Data Mining detects outliers across a vast amount of data. The criminal data includes all details of the crime that has happened. Data Mining will study the patterns and trends and predict future events with better accuracy.

The agencies can find out which area is more prone to crime, how much police personnel should be deployed, which age group should be targeted, vehicle numbers to be scrutinised, etc.

Forecasting Crime Incidents using Cluster Analysis and Bayesian Belief Networks

Data mining is a promising tool in the fight against terrorism and crime. It plays a number of important roles in counter terrorism including locating known suspects, identifying and tracking suspicious financial and other transactions, and facilitating background checks.

Data mining in the context of crime and intelligence analysis for national security is still a young field. The following describes the applications of different techniques in crime data mining.

Entity extraction has been used to automatically identify person, address, vehicle, narcotic drug, and personal properties from police narrative reports

Clustering techniques such as "concept space" have been used to automatically associate different objects (such as persons, organisations, vehicles) in crime records.

Deviation Detection has been applied in fraud detection, network intrusion detection, and other crime analyses that involve tracing abnormal activities.

Classification has been used to detect email spamming and find authors who send out unsolicited emails.

String comparators have been used to detect deceptive information in criminal records.

Social network analysis has been used to analyse criminals" roles and associations among entities in a criminal network.

Crime Data mining

1.Named-Entity Extraction
Most criminal justice databases capture only structured data that fits in predefined fields. The first data mining task involved extracting named entities from police narrative reports, which are difficult to analyse using automated investigators in crime analysis. It proposed a neural network-based entity extractor, which applies named-entity extraction techniques to automatically identify useful entities from police narrative reports.

The system has three major components:
(1) Noun phrasing: It is a modified version of the Arizona Noun Phraser and extracts noun phrases as named entities from documents based on syntactical analysis;

(2) Finite state machine and lexical lookup: A finite state machine compares each word in the extracted phrase, as well as the words immediately before and after the phrase, with the items in a hand crafted lexicon. Each comparison will generate a binary value (either 0 or 1) to indicate a match or mismatch;

(3) Neural network: The feedforward/backpropagation neural network predicts the most likely entity type for each phrase.

2. Deceptive Identity Detection:An Algorithmic Approach

Criminals often provide police officers with deceptive identities to mislead police investigations, for example, using aliases, fabricated birth dates or addresses, etc. The large amount of data also prevents officers from examining inexact matches manually.

The second data mining task involves automatically detecting deceptive criminal identities from the police departments databases, which contains information such as name, gender, address, ID number, and physical description.It was found that criminals usually made minor changes to their real identity information.

Based on the taxonomy,an algorithmic approach was developed to detect deceptive criminal identities automatically. This approach utilised four identity fields: name, address, date-of birth, and social security- number and compared each corresponding field for a pair of criminal identity records.

The method employees string comparators to compare values in the corresponding fields of each record pair. Comparators measure the similarity between two strings. An overall disagreement value between the two records was computed by calculating the Euclidean Distance of disagreement measures over all attribute fields. A Euclidean vector norm is the square root of the sum of squared similarity measures and is also normalise between 0 and 1. The algorithm could accurately detect 94% of criminal identity deceptions

3. Criminal Network Analysis

Criminals often develop networks in which they form groups or teams to carry out various illegal organised crimes such as narcotics trafficking, terrorism, gang-related crimes, and frauds. The fourth data mining task consists of identifying subgroups and key members in such networks and then studying interaction patterns to develop effective strategies for disrupting the networks. Social Network Analysis (SNA) has been recognized as an appropriate methodology to uncover previously unknown structural patterns from criminal networks

Four steps are involved in this task:

(1) **Network extraction**: It utilises crime incident reports as sources for criminal relationship information because criminals who committed crimes together usually were related. The concept space approach is used to identify and uncover criminal relationships;

(2) **Sub group Detection**: It employs hierarchical clustering to detect subgroups in a criminal network based on relational strength;

(3) **Interaction pattern discovery:** It employs an SNA approach called block modelling to reveal patterns of between-group interaction. Given a partitioned network, block model analysis determines the presence or absence of an interaction between a pair of subgroups by comparing the density of the links between these two subgroups to a pre defined threshold value;

(4) **Central member identification:** It employs several measures, such as degree, between-ness, and closeness to identify central members in a given subgroup. These three measures can suggest the centrality of a network member.

4. Authorship Analysis in Cybercrime

The next data mining task proposes an authorship analysis framework to automatically trace identities of cyber criminals through messages they post on the Internet. Under this framework, three types of message features, including style markers, structural features, and content-specific features, are extracted and inductive learning algorithms are used to build feature-based models to identify authorship of illegal messages. The experimental results indicated a promising future of using our framework to address the identity-tracing problem.

Crime Data Mining with Clustering Techniques

Clustering is another data mining technique that can be used to detect crime and terrorism. Clustering techniques and algorithms are based on real-life models that individuals with certain qualities must cluster together.

A crime data analyst or detective will use a report based on this data sorted in different orders, usually the first

Crime Type	Suspect Race	Suspect Sex	Suspect Age group	Victim Age group	Weapons
Robbery	B	M	Middel	Elderly	Knife
Robbery	W	M	Young	Middel	Bat
Robbery	B	M	?	Elderly	Knife
Robbery	B	F	Middel	Young	Piston

The type of crime is robbery and it will be the most important attribute. The rows 1 and 3 show a simple crime pattern where the suspect description matches and the victim profile is also similar. The aim here is that we can use data mining to detect much more complex patterns since in real life there are many attributes or factors for crime and often there is partial information available about the crime.

Thus, Clustering techniques using data mining come in handy to deal with enormous amounts of data and dealing with noisy or missing data about crime incidents.

The technique used here is **k-means clustering** as it is one of the most widely used data mining clustering techniques. Next, the most important part is to prepare the data for the analysis. The operational data is converted into denormalized data using the extraction and transformation. Then, some checks are run to look at the quality of data such as missing data, outliers and multiple abbreviations for the same word such as blank, unknown, or junk all meant the same for missing age of the person.

The next task is to identify the significant attributes for the clustering. This process involves talking to domain experts such as the crime detectives, the crime data analysts and iteratively running the attribute importance algorithm to arrive at the set of attributes for the clustering of the given crime types. This is referred to as the semi-supervised or expert-based paradigm of problem solving.

Based on the nature of crime the different attributes become important such as the age group of victim is important for homicide, for burglary the same may not be as important since the burglar may not care about the age of the owner of the house.

To take care of the different attributes for different crime types, the concept of weighing the attributes was introduced. Based on the weighted clustering attributes,the dataset is clustered for crime patterns and then the result is presented to the detective or the domain expert along with the statistics of the important attributes. This iterative process helps to determine the significant attributes and the weights for different crime types.

Based on this information from the domain expert, namely the detective, future crime patterns can be detected.

Source - https://www.ijert.org/research/effective-data-mining-approach-for-crime-terrorpattern-detection-using-clustering-algorithm-technique-IJERTV2IS4943.pdf

Note : Data mining is not about reading data from directory like lookup phone number in phone directory or Expert system in AI (Expert system takes decision on experience of designed algorithm) or Simple SQL queries to retrieve data from multiple tables.

What Kind of data can mines

Data mining is not specific to one media or data type. Data mining should be applicable to any kind of data repository. However, data mining algorithms and approaches may differ based on the nature of data and its types. Data mining is used to study different databases including relational databases, data warehouses, flat files, transactional databases, unstructured and semi structured databases such as WWW (World Wide Web), multimedia databases and time-series databases etc. Here are some examples in detail.

- **Flat file**: is a text or binary data file with a structure that data mining algorithms can easily extract. It is the most common data source for data mining. The data in these files can be transactions, time-series data, scientific measurements, etc.

- **Relational Database:** is a data collection of a set of tables with rows and columns. In most of the relational databases SQL query language, which allows retrieval and manipulation of the data stored in the tables, as well as the calculation purpose such as aggregate functions, cum, min, max, count.

- **Data Warehouse**: A data warehouse as a storehouse, is a repository of data collected from multiple data sources (often heterogeneous) and is intended to be used as a whole under the same unified schema. A data warehouse gives the option to analyse data from different sources under the same roof. Data warehouses consist of three types, enterprise data warehouses, data marts, and virtual warehouses. It is widely used in everyday business decision-making.

- **A Transaction Database**: is a set of records representing transactions, each transaction is with a time stamp, an identifier and a set of items. One common example for transactional data includes your online shopping through e-commerce sites. Typical data mining analysis on such transaction data is the so-called market basket analysis or association rules in which associations between items occurring together or in sequence are studied.

- **Multimedia Databases**: Multimedia databases include video, images, audio and text media. They can be stored on extended object-relational or object-oriented databases, or simply on a file system. Multimedia is characterised by its high dimensionality, which makes data mining even more challenging. Data mining from multimedia repositories may require computer vision, computer graphics, image interpretation, and natural language processing methodologies.

- **Spatial Databases**: Spatial databases are databases that, in addition to usual data, store geographical information like maps, and global or regional positioning. Such spatial databases present new challenges to data mining algorithms.

- **Time-Series Databases:** Time-series databases contain time related data such as stock market data or logged activities. These databases usually have a continuous flow of new data coming in, which sometimes causes the need for a challenging real time analysis. Data mining in such databases commonly includes the study of trends and correlations between evolutions of different variables, as well as the prediction of trends and movements of the variables in time. Figure 1.7 shows some examples of time-series data.

- **World Wide Web:** The World Wide Web is the most heterogeneous and dynamic repository available. A very large number of authors and publishers are continuously contributing to its growth and metamorphosis, and a massive number of users are accessing its resources daily. Data in the world wide web is organised in inter-connected documents. These documents can be text, audio, video, raw data, and even applications. Conceptually, the world wide web comprises three major components: The content of the web, which encompasses documents available; the structure of the web, which covers the hyperlinks and the relationships between documents; and the usage of the web, describing how and when the resources are accessed. A fourth dimension can be added relating the dynamic nature or evolution of the documents. Data mining in the world wide web, or web mining, tries to address all these issues and is often divided into web content mining, web structure mining and web usage mining.

How does Data Mining work ?

The data mining process involves a number of steps from data collection to visualisation to extract valuable information from large data sets. There are about as many approaches to data mining depending on the kind of questions being asked and organisation data. As mentioned above, data mining techniques are used to generate descriptions and predictions about a target data set.

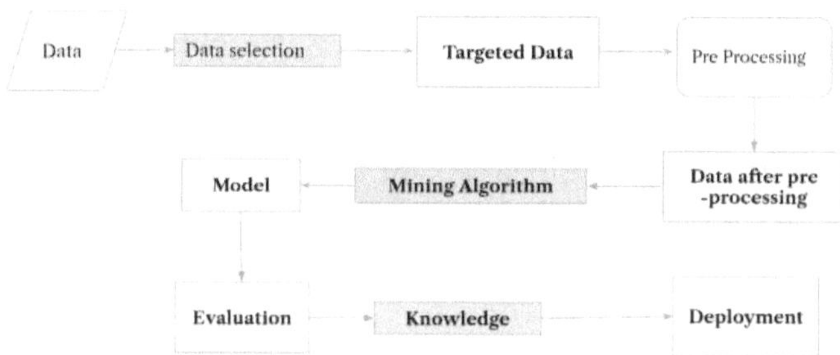

- **Identifying business goals**: What business problem are you trying to solve? Customer Acquisition? Retention? Reduce maintenance costs or operational costs? This can be the hardest part of the data mining process, and many organisations spend too little time on this important step. Data scientists and business stakeholders need to work together to define the business problem, which helps inform the data questions and parameters for a given project.

- **Data Collection and Preparation:** Once business objectives are clear, it's important to identify key data sources, either internal or external dataset. You may need to integrate with multiple data sources. Once data is collected it has to be cleaned, removed and transformed into the right business entities or dimensions. The data preparation process can be divided into three parts: data selection, data pre-processing, and data transmission.

- **Data Mining Engine**: Data mining engine is the core part of the data mining system. A set of functional modules or tools compose the data mining engine that each functional module consists of several data mining algorithms and rules such as data summary, classification, clustering, association rule discovery, or sequential pattern discovery, that is, to decide what type of data mining method to use.

- **Modelling:** Actual Data mining starts with the model building step. Depending upon business use cases data mining algorithms or techniques can be used such as sequential patterns, association rules or correlation. Depending upon supervised learning or unsupervised learning algorithms could differ.

- **Evaluation:** Evaluate preliminary results and test the model on different sample data sets and review the results. Do these results across different samples correlate? Are there any inconsistencies? Keep iterating until you are satisfied with the consistency of the results.

- **Deployment:** Run the analysis and make the results of the project available to decision makers. Remember that data mining is as much about story-telling as it is about modelling. Report the findings and operationalize the process.

Throughout this process, we need a close collaboration among different experts like Data Scientist, Data Engineers and Business Analysts (Domain experts).

Data mining techniques

Data mining works by using various algorithms and techniques to turn large volumes of data into useful information. Here are some of the most common ones:

Data mining techniques can be categorically into:

- **Descriptive model:** Descriptive analytics finds patterns and relationships in current data.

- **Predictive model:** Used to predict future outcomes, such as whether a loan applicant is a good risk, or to make financial forecasts, such as upcoming sales.

- **Outlier Analysis:** Used to find anomalies, that is, data that doesn't fit neatly into patterns. Outlier analysis is especially useful in fraud detection, network intrusion detection and criminal investigations

Association rules

An association rule is a rule-based method for finding relationships between variables in a given dataset. These methods are frequently used for market basket analysis, allowing companies to better understand relationships between different products. Understanding the consumption habits of customers enables businesses to develop better cross-selling strategies and recommendation engines.

- For retailers, it's particularly helpful in making purchasing suggestions. For example, if a customer buys a smartphone, tablet, or video game device, association analysis can recommend related items like cables, applicable software, and protective cases.

Neural networks

Primarily leveraged for deep learning algorithms, neural networks process training data by mimicking the interconnectivity of the human brain through layers of nodes. Each node is made up of inputs, weights, a bias (or threshold), and an output. If that output value exceeds a given threshold, it "fires" or activates the node, passing data to the next layer in the network. Neural networks learn this mapping function through supervised learning, adjusting based on the loss function through the process of gradient descent. When the cost function is at or near zero, we can be confident in the model's accuracy to yield the correct answer.

- Neural networks have a wide range of applications. They can help businesses predict consumer buying patterns and focus marketing campaigns on specific demographics. They can also help retailers make accurate sales forecasts and understand how to use dynamic pricing. Furthermore, they help to improve diagnostic and treatment methods in healthcare, improving care and performance.

Clustering

To help users understand the natural groupings or structure within the data, you can apply the process of partitioning a dataset into a set of meaningful sub-classes called clusters. This process looks at all the objects in the dataset and groups them together based on similarity to each other, rather than on predetermined features.

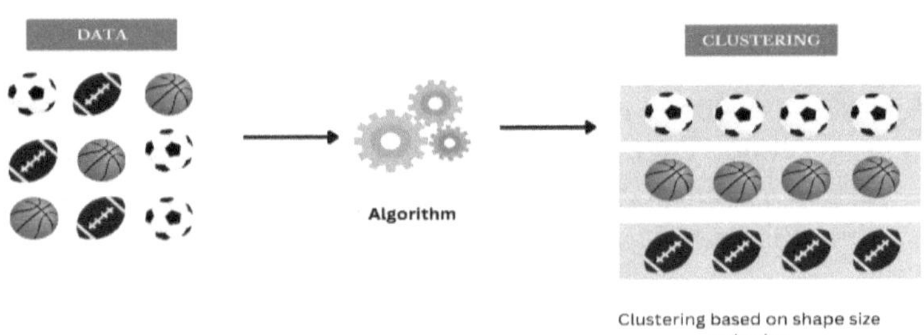

Clustering based on shape size
and color

- For example, retailers can use clustering models to determine which customers buy particular products, on which days, and with what frequency. This can help retailers target products and services to customers in a specific demographic or region.

Classification

classification is considered to be a form of clustering. This technique sorts items in a dataset into different target categories or classes based on common features. This allows the algorithm to neatly categorise even complex data cases. Classification is also used to designate broad groups within a demographic, target audience, or user base through which businesses can gain stronger insights.

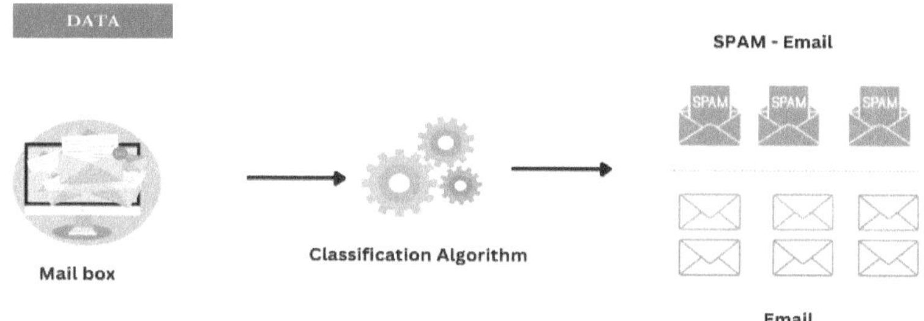

- Financial institutions classify consumers based on many variables to market new loans or project credit card risks. Meanwhile, weather apps classify data to project snowfall totals and other similar figures. Grocery stores also use classification to group products by the consumers who buy them, helping forecast buying patterns.

Different methods under Data Mining Classification includes

- **Logistic regression:** This algorithm attempts to show the probability of a specific outcome within two possible results. For example, an email service can use logistic regression to predict whether or not an email is spam.

- **Decision tree:** This data mining technique uses classification or regression methods to classify or predict potential outcomes based on a set of decisions. As the name suggests, it uses a tree-like visualisation to represent the potential outcomes of these decisions.

  - For example, if a computer company wants to predict the likelihood of laptop purchases, it may ask, Is the potential buyer a student? '' The data is classified into "Yes" and "No" decision trees, with other questions to be asked afterward in a similar fashion.

- **K-nearest neighbours (KNN):** K-nearest neighbour, also known as the KNN algorithm, is a non-parametric algorithm that classifies data points based on their proximity and association to other available data. This algorithm assumes that similar data points can be found near each other. As a result, it seeks to calculate the distance between data points, usually through euclidean distance, and then it assigns a category based on the most frequent category or average. For instance, grocery chains might use the K-nearest neighbours algorithm to decide whether to include a sushi or hot meals station in their new store layout based on consumer habits in the local marketplace.

- **Naive Bayes:** Based on the Bayes Theorem of Probability, this algorithm uses historical data to predict whether similar events will occur based on a different set of data.

- **Support Vector Machine (SVM):** This machine learning algorithm is often used to define the line that best divides a data set into two classes. An SVM can help classify images and is used in facial and handwriting recognition software.

Outlier Detection

While other data mining methods seek to identify patterns and trends, outlier detection looks for the unique: the data point or points that differ from the rest or diverge from the overall sample. Outlier detection finds errors, such as data that was input incorrectly or extracted from the wrong sample. Natural data deviations can be instructive as well.

- Example: Retailers can use outlier detection to learn why their stores witness an odd increase in purchases, such as snow shovels being bought in the summer, and how to respond to such findings.

Generally, outlier detection is employed to enhance logistics, instil a culture of preemptive damage control, and create a smoother environment for customers, users, and other key groups.

Methods used for Outlier Detection:

- **Numeric outlier:** Outliers are detected based on the Interquartile Range, or the middle 50 percent of values. Data points outside that range are considered outliers.

- **Z-score:** The Z-Score denotes how many standard deviations a data point is from the sample's mean. This is also known as extreme value analysis.

- **DBSCAN**: This stands for "density-based spatial clustering of applications with noise" and is a method that defines data as core points, border points, and noise points, which are the outliers.

- **Isolation forest:** This method isolates anomalies in large sets of data (the forest) with an algorithm that searches for those anomalies instead of profiling normal data points.

Prediction Modelling

Predictive modelling is among the most common uses of data mining and works best with large data sets that represent a broad sample size.

Predictive models can be built to determine sales projections and predict consumer buying habits. They help manufacturers forecast distribution needs and determine maintenance schedules. Government agencies use census data to map population trends and project spending needs while baseball teams use predictive models to determine contracts and build rosters.

Methods for prediction:

Predictive modelling uses some of the same techniques and terminology as other data mining processes. Here are four examples:

- **Forecast modelling:** This is a common technique in which the computer answers a question (for instance, How much milk should a store have in stock on Monday?) by analysing historical data.

- **Classification modelling:** Classification places data into groups where it can be used to answer direct questions.

- **Cluster modelling:** By clustering data into groups with shared characteristics, a predictive model can be used to study those data sets and make decisions.

- **Time series modelling:** This model analyses data based on when the data was input. A study of sales trends over a year is an example of time series modelling.

Data Mining Challenges

Data mining is a widely accepted technique and used by many organisations. Data mining involve with modern tools and techniques, however data mining not able to handle all the issues, It has some major challenges, some of them are handled below:

Data Source Issues: Typically, in a traditional system, data is stored in multiple databases in a distributed environment. It is very important to combine all the data into one central data store. But combining data from multiple sources into a central data store is very challenging, it requires data to translate into common definition and standard format, which is very tedious and time-consuming tasks. There are many issues related to the data sources. General practice across industry to collect as much data as you can but handling such excess data is challenging since we already have more data than we can handle and we are still collecting data at an even higher rate.

Data Incompletion: Data mining works with immense volume of data. Data can be at different types and from different sources. Data quality is key attributes for the right decision; however, data noise is a major challenge. Inconsistent and incomplete data leads to faulty analysis and irrational decisions.

Data Security: Major issue with data mining is with data security and privacy. Data transmission and sharing demand extra security. Data collection process might collect personal or sensitive information and it should restrict to unauthorised users, and maintain confidentiality of information.

Scalability and Performance: With exponential growth in data size, scalability is a challenge for both storage and computation. Scalability of algorithms depends on the volume of the data.
Many statistical and mining algorithms exist in the analytical world however those algorithms are not designed for handling huge volumes of data, terabytes of data. Performance of a data mining system depends primarily on the efficiency of the algorithm techniques used. Algorithms with exponential or polynomial complexity cannot be used efficiently.

Visual Presentation: Good data visualisation eases the interpretation of data mining results, as well as helps users better understand the data. There are many visualisation ideas and proposals for effective data presentation. However, handling complex data is an issue with visual graphics. Not all visualisation libraries cope with such huge volume and complexity.

Web Mining

Web mining is data mining techniques used to extract information from multiple websites. This is an automatic process. For discovering useful data (videos, tables, audio, images etc.) from the web different techniques and tools are used. Information over the internet is huge and increasing with passage to time due to which size of databases are also growing.

Different tools and techniques are used for extraction of data from web pages that includes web documents, images, hyperlinks, usage logs etc.

Web Mining Categories

Web mining is categorised into three types:

- Web Content Mining
- Web Structure Mining
- Web Usage Mining

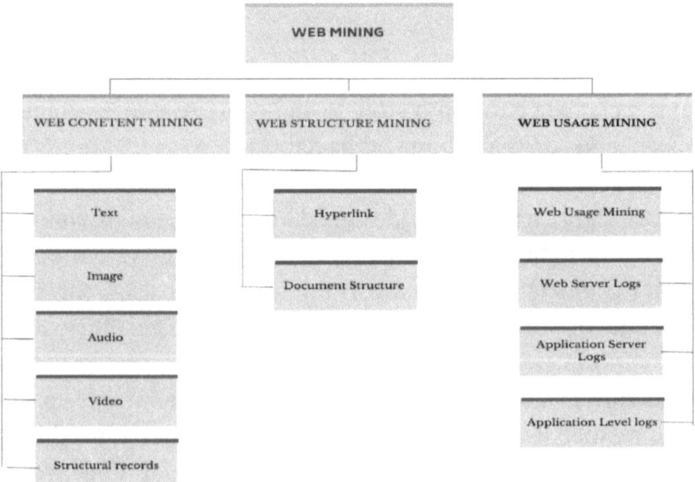

Mining Category	Techniques
Web Content Mining	• Web Page Content Mining • Search result mining
Web Structure Mining	• Hyperlink Structure • Document Structure
Web Usage Mining	• General Access Pattern Tracking • Customised Usage pattern tracking

Web Content Mining

Web Content mining deals with knowledge of the web content like text, image, audio, video, metadata, hyperlinks and extracts useful information. Web mining helps to understand customer behaviour, helps to evaluate the performance of a web site and the research done in web content mining indirectly helps to boost business.

Web content mining examines the content of the web as well as the result of the search. It can be further classified into web page content mining and search result mining.

Web Content Mining includes following techniques

Structural Data	• Web Crawler • Wrapper Generation • Page Content mining
Unstructured Data	• Information Extraction • Topic Tracking • Summarization • Categorization • Clustering • Information Visualisation

Semi Structured Data

- Object Exchange Model
- Top-Down extraction
- Web Data Extraction Language

Web Structure Mining

Web Structure Mining offers information about how different pages are linked together to form this huge web. Web Structure Mining finds hidden basic structures and uses hyperlinks for more web applications such as web search.

In the business world, structure mining can be quite useful in determining the connection between two or more business websites. The determined connection brings forth a useful tool for mapping competing companies through third party links such as resellers and customers.

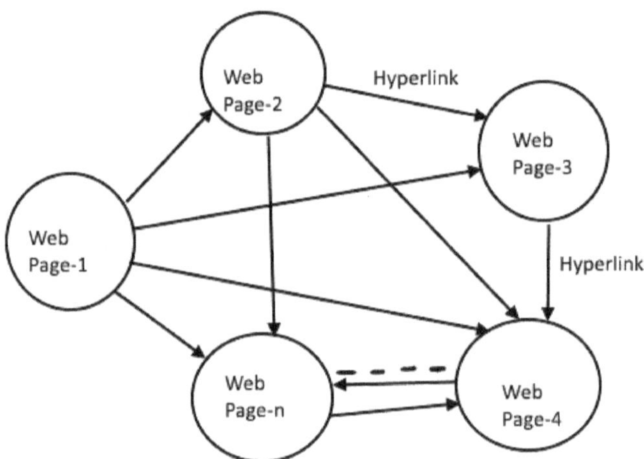

Web structure mining can be further divided into two kinds based on the kind of structure information used.

- **Hyperlinks:** A hyperlink is a structural unit that connects a location in a web page to a different location, either within the same web page or on a different web page. A hyperlink that connects to a different part of the same page is called an intra-document hyperlink, and a hyperlink that connects two different pages is called an inter-document hyperlink.

- **Document Structure:** The content within a web page can also be organised in a tree-structured format, based on the various HTML and XML tags within the page. Mining efforts have focused on automatically extracting document object model (DOM) structures out of documents.

Web mining and the use of structure mining can provide strategic results for marketing of a website for production of sale. The more traffic directed to the web pages of a particular site increases the level of return visitation to the site and recall by search engines relating to the information or product provided by the company.

Web Usage Mining

Web usage mining is to identify the browsing patterns by analysing the navigational behaviour of the user. It focuses on techniques that can be used to predict the user behaviour while the user interacts with the web. It uses the secondary data on the web. This activity involves automatic discovery of user access patterns from one or more web- servers. It consists of three phases namely: pre-processing, pattern discovery, pattern analysis.web usage mining itself can be classified further depending on the kind of usage data considered: Web Server Data, Web Server Data, Application Level Data.

- **Web Server Data** The user logs are collected by the Web server. Typical data includes IP address, page reference and access time.

- **Application Server:** Data Commercial application servers have significant features to enable e-commerce applications to be built on top of them with little effort. A key feature is the ability to track various kinds of business events and log them in application server logs.

- **Application Level Data:** New kinds of events can be defined in an application, and logging can be turned on for them thus generating histories of these specially defined events. It must be noted, however, that many end applications require a combination of one or more of the techniques applied in the categories above.

Summary

This chapter covers basic understanding of data mining and its techniques. Key understanding includes following points:

- Data mining aims to understand and discover new, previously unseen knowledge in the data.

- The data mining process involves a number of steps data collection, data preparation, model building, evaluation and deployment

- Common data mining techniques includes,

    - Association rule,
    - Neural networks,
    - Clustering
    - Classification
    - Outlier Detection
    - Predictive Modelling

- Data Mining is widely used in different industries for the betterment of humankind.

- WIth increase in high volume of data, data mining faces scalability and security challenges.

- Web Mining is a technique used to extract information from multiple websites.

- Mining techniques include content mining, structure mining and usage mining.

References

- https://webdocs.cs.ualberta.ca/~zaiane/courses/cmput690/notes/Chapter1/
- https://www.ibm.com/cloud/learn/data-mining
- https://bootcamp.pe.gatech.edu/blog/10-key-data-mining-techniques-and-how-businesses-use-them/
- https://www.ijert.org/web-content-mining-techniques-a-comprehensive-survey
- https://www.researchgate.net/figure/Web-structure-mining-as-a-graph_fig2_305993898
- https://www.raconteur.net/technology/actionable-data-for-enterprise-decision-making/

Six

Let machine understand your data-AI/ML

"Someone on TV has only to say, 'Alexa,' and she lights up. She's always ready for action, the perfect woman, never says, "Not tonight, dear."

—Sybil Sage, as quoted in a New York Times article

Introduction

Everyone of us uses AI in some form, AI is part of our everyday life, for example, talking to your smartphone requires the use of speech recognition AI. AI does perform a significant number of useful tasks. Artificial intelligence allows machines to replicate the capabilities of the human mind. From the development of self-driving cars to the proliferation of smart assistants like Siri and Alexa, AI is a growing part of everyday life. As a result, many tech companies across various industries are investing in artificially intelligent technologies.

No matter how much data you have, you still need an algorithm to make it useful. An algorithm is a procedure, which is a sequence of operations, usually dealt with by a computer that guarantees to find the correct solution to the problem.

AI and machine learning are new innovative approaches for business drivers and many organisations are adopting it as part of their digital transformation.

What is Artificial Intelligence?

Artificial intelligence is a wide-ranging branch of computer science concerned with building smart machines capable of performing tasks that typically require human intelligence.

A Day in the Life of AI

Unknowingly most of us use AI, starting from unlocking our phone using facial recognition to Netflix recommendation to spell check in out text. Some examples are highlighted below for better understanding.

Speaking Smart Assistance: Alexa and Siri are good examples of voice recognition and perform specific tasks. Voice recognition softwares breaks the sound into words and phrases. Those words are mapped with available datasets. Algorithms are built to identify the right set of instructions and execute specific tasks.

Blocking unwanted emails: Identify spam, non spam emails in gmail, rely on deep learning techniques. Algorithms learn from the users click behaviour, "Report spam" or "Not Spam" and some filter patterns and keywords. Gmail uses a neural network to filter out phishing attempts.

Spell check: Composing email is very easy. Grammarly and gmail introduced algorithms that assists users for guessing the next phrase of text and spot error while writing.

Unlock phone: First thing most of us do as soon as we wake up in the morning is to unlock your phone. Just looking at the phone it gets unlocked. Using AI algorithms, face recognition helps to build this capability in phones.

Netflix Recommendation: Assist users for effortless shopping experience by avoiding search operation. Based on the customer history data and patterns or similar customer purchasing habits, Netflix recommends a product list.

Stages of Artificial Intelligence

Artificial intelligence has a lot of potential to grow, some stages are still undiscovered and the research is going on. Artificial intelligence can be categorised into three stages, depending upon the role they play. In this section, we will go through all of these stages, including their real-world application.

- Artificial Narrow Intelligence (ANI)
- Artificial General Intelligence (AGI)
- Artificial Super Intelligence (ASI)

Artificial Narrow Intelligence (ANI) : The name suggests, it is limited in scope with intelligence restricted to only one functional area. It is also known as Weak AI. Artificial Intelligence involves machines that perform only narrowly defined specific tasks. Machines don't possesses any thinking capability they only perform given tasks

Currently, all AI activities involve under this category some examples include Alexa, Siri, or self driving cars etc.

Let's consider an example of a virtual assistant such as Siri, Alexa, and Google Assistant. All these virtual assistants are programmed in such a way that they can perform several tasks, but these tasks are limited only to their respective devices, i.e., smartphones, tablets, etc.

Artificial General Intelligence (AGI): Also known as Strong AI, AGI would mean a machine would be capable of understanding the world as well as any human. All this while maintaining the same capacity to learn how to carry out a huge range of tasks. AGI is not yet among us. It is a hypothetical form of AI.

Artificial Super Intelligence (ASI): ASI is the stage of Artificial intelligence when the capability of machines will suppress humans. It is currently in hypothetical form and only seen in friction movies.

Domains of Artificial Intelligence (AI)

Domains are the different areas in which artificial intelligence technology can be used. Artificial intelligence technology can be used to create and interpret text, images, and other forms of information.

- Machine Learning
- Deep Learning
- Robotics
- Expert Systems
- Fuzzy Logic
- Natural Language Processing
- Computer vision

Machine Learning

Machine Learning is a subset of artificial intelligence. Machine learning focuses on the development of computer programs that can access data and use it to learn for themselves rather than being explicitly programmed for a certain task.

"Machine learning algorithms are used in a wide variety of applications, such as in medicine, email filtering, speech recognition, and computer vision, where it is difficult or unfeasible to develop conventional algorithms to perform tasks." - Wikipedia

Machine learning models are used in medical diagnosis, image processing, prediction, classification, learning association, regression etc.

Machine learning classifiers fall into three primary categories:

1. Supervised learning
2. Unsupervised learning
3. Reinforcement learning

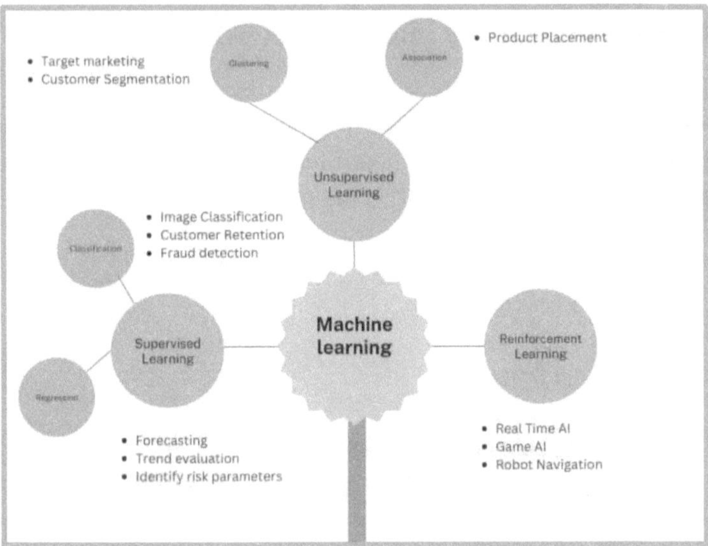

4.

Supervised learning:

As humans, we consume a lot of information, knowingly and unknowingly it is stored in our memory but often don't notice these data points. When we see a photo of an animal, for example, we instantly know what the animal is based on our prior experience. But what happens when the learner doesn't instantly recognize the animal?

When the learner makes a guess and predicts what the animal might be, we have the opportunity to objectively evaluate whether the learner has given a correct answer or not. This is possible because we have the correct labels of input.

From now on, we'll be referring to the machine learning algorithm as "the model". Now, if the model gave a correct answer, then there is nothing for us to do. Our job is to correct the model when the output of the model is wrong. If this is the case, we need to make sure that the model makes necessary updates so that the next time a cat image is shown to the model, it can correctly identify the image.

The formal supervised learning process involves input variables, which we call (X), and an output variable, which we call (Y). We use an algorithm to learn the mapping function from the input to the output. In simple mathematics, the output (Y) is a dependent variable of input (X) as illustrated by:

$Y = f(X)$

Supervised Learning in ML

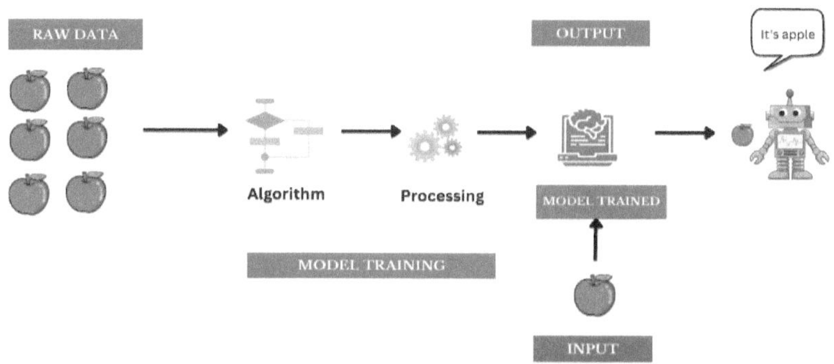

Example: How's the weather today?

One interesting problem which requires considering a lot of different parameters is predicting weather conditions in a particular location. To make correct predictions for the weather, we need to take into account various parameters, including historical temperature data, precipitation, wind, humidity, and so on.

This particularly interesting and challenging problem may require developing complex supervised models that include multiple tasks. Predicting today's temperature is a regression problem, where the output labels are continuous variables. By contrast, predicting whether it is going to snow or not tomorrow is a binary classification problem.

Supervised machine learning can be classified into two types of problems:

- Classification
- Regression

> **Hopper - A Travel Partner**
>
> Hopper is an accredited travel agency. Hopper partners with airlines, hotels, homes, and car rental providers across the globe so you can feel confident you're booking the perfect vacation at the best price.
>
> Hopper uses AI to predict when you should be able to book the lowest prices for flights, hotels, car and vacation home rentals. The company's AI scans hundreds of bookings and presents the most up-to-date prices. But, there's so much more to this AI.

Unsupervised Learning

Unsupervised learning is different from supervised learning, as the name suggests there is no need for supervision. Unsupervised learning tries to find the hidden structures in unlabelled data. The learner is provided only with input without known outputs, while learning is performed by finding similarities in the input data.

We do this kind of learning everyday. In unsupervised learning, even though we do not have any labels for data points but we do have actual data points. We can draw the references from observations in the input data.

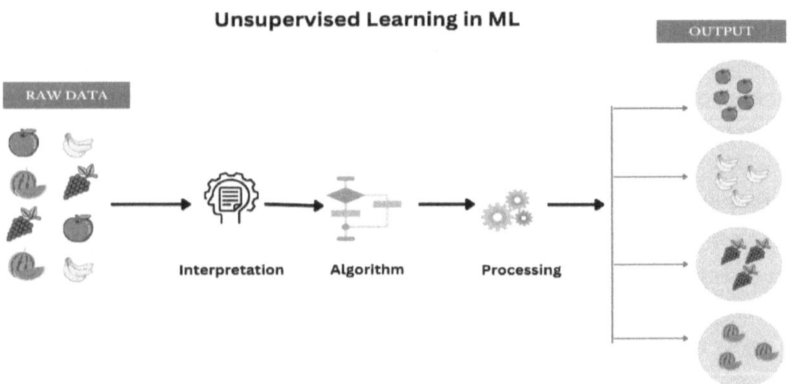

The main aim of the unsupervised learning algorithm is to group or categorise the unsorted dataset according to the similarities, patterns, and differences. Machines are instructed to find the hidden patterns from the input dataset.

Let's take an example to understand it more precisely; suppose there is a basket of fruit images, and we put it into the machine learning model. The images are totally unknown to the model, and the task of the machine is to find the patterns and categories of the objects.

So, now the machine will discover its patterns and differences, such as colour difference, and shape difference, and predict the output when it is tested with the test dataset.

Unsupervised machine learning can be classified into two types of problems:

- Clustering
- Association

Reinforcement learning

Reinforcement learning is a type of machine learning in which a computer learns to perform a task through repeated trial and error interaction with a dynamic environment. This learning approach enables the computer to make a series of decisions that maximise a reward metric for the tasks without human intervention and without being explicitly programmed to achieve the task.

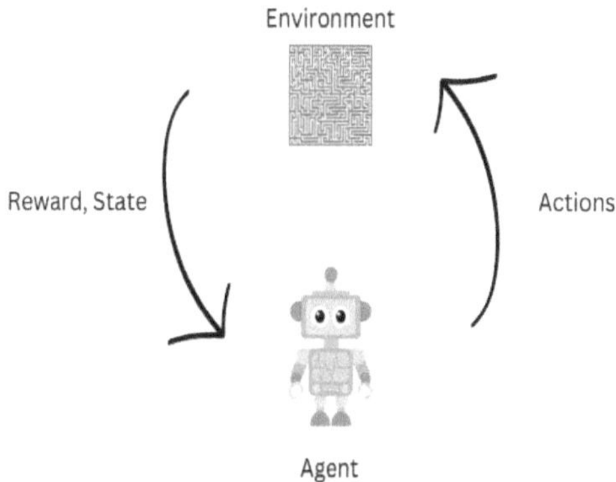

Machine Learning Use Cases:

- Robot Navigation
- Game AI

Waymo - Self Driving Car

Waymo LLC, formerly known as the Google self-driving car project, is an American autonomous driving technology company headquartered in Mountain View, California. It is a subsidiary of Alphabet Inc, the parent company of Google. The company builds a variety of autonomous vehicles designed to meet the needs of drivers, including individuals, rideshare drivers and large trucking companies.

Waymo's vehicles have already driven millions of miles across more than 10 states, using AI along the way to collect and analyse data. With an advanced suite of sensors, each Waymo vehicle collects data and uses artificial intelligence to decipher what will happen next.

Deep Learning

Deep Learning is an artificial intelligence (AI) function that imitates the working of the human brain in processing data and creating patterns for use in decision making.

Deep learning is a subset of machine learning in artificial intelligence that has a network capable of learning unsupervised from data that is unstructured or unlabelled also known as deep neural learning or deep neural network.

In deep learning, a computer model learns to perform classification tasks directly from images, text, or sound. Deep learning models can achieve state-of-the-art accuracy, sometimes exceeding human-level performance. Models are trained by using a large set of labelled data and neural network architectures that contain many layers.

Different types of deep learning models:

1. Autoencoders
2. Deep belief net
3. Convolutional neural network
4. Recurrent neural network
5. Reinforcement learning to neural network

Robotics

Robotics: It is a branch of engineering that involves the conception, design, manufacture, and operation of robots. This field overlaps with electronics, computer science, artificial intelligence, mechatronics, nanotechnology and bioengineering.

Different types of robots:

1. Pre-programmed robots
2. Humanoid robots
3. Autonomous robots
4. Teleoperated robots
5. Augmenting robots

Pre-programmed robots: These are the ones that have to be told ahead of time what to do, and then they simply execute that program. They cannot change their behaviour while they are working, and no human is guiding their actions.

There are pre-programmed robotic arms, so large that they are able to handle entire automobiles as if they were toy cars. There are also pre-programmed robots that can make the tiniest weld or spray paint with aesthetic precision. Manufacturing has never been the same since robots have taken over the jobs that humans used to do.

Humanoid robots: Humanoid robots are professional service robots built to mimic human motion and interaction. Like all service robots, they provide value by automating tasks in a way that leads to cost-savings and productivity.

Humanoid robots are being used in the inspection, maintenance and disaster response at power plants to relieve human workers of laborious and dangerous tasks.

Sophia - Humanoid robot

Sophia is a social humanoid robot developed by the Hong Kong-based company Hanson Robotics. Through AI, Sophia can efficiently communicate with natural language and use facial expressions to convey human-like emotions.

Sophia has become something of a media celebrity, featured on various talk shows, including a memorable appearance with a clearly weirded-out Jimmy Fallon on The Tonight Show. The robot has even accepted citizenship from Saudi Arabia.

Autonomous robots: Autonomous medical robots are able to operate intelligently and adapt to their environment without direct human supervision. In particular, they should be able to perform their duties in an environment that might be changing, and without a person sitting at a bank of controls directing their activities.

High-Tech 'TUG' Robots

A TUG is an autonomous mobile robot made specifically for hospitals by Aethon, a company based in Pittsburgh. It uses a built-in map and sensors to navigate hospital halls and communicates with elevators, fire alarms and automatic doors via Wi-Fi.

TUG was designed with nurses in mind. With TUG, nurses know when meds, meals, supplies and tests are arriving. No more chasing. No more calling. No kidding. The result is higher job satisfaction and more time for patient care.

TUG securely delivers medications through the hospital and directly to nursing units. It secures and automates deliveries that are normally made through pneumatic tubes or manual couriers including controlled substances and refilling carts.

TUG provides automated, cost-effective delivery of meals to patient floors and returns dirty trays to Food Service. With TUG, staff can spend more time managing dietary needs and interacting with patients.

TUG is a safer, more efficient way to manage waste removal. The system also integrates automated dumping equipment so the cart can empty without employee assistance which is especially useful after hours.

Teleoperated robots: Teleoperated robots are controlled remotely by a human being. The remote control signals can be sent through a wire, through a local wireless system (like Wi-Fi), over the Internet or by satellite.

Teleoperated robots are mostly used in medical surgeries and military operations. Critical surgeries are made easier with teleoperated robotic arms or tools due to their ability to reach the tightest places where human hands can't operate. In military operations, teleoperated robots help to gather Intel and perform dangerous tasks like diffusing or moving an explosive. Until recently, these teleoperated robots used to be controlled by a joystick style setup or console-like controllers, pretty similar to what you have on your PlayStation, Xbox or Wii consoles

Da-Vinci
The Da Vinci surgical system gives your surgeon an advanced set of instruments to use in performing robotic-assisted minimally invasive surgery. The term "robotic" often misleads people. Robots don't perform surgery. Your surgeon performs surgery with Da Vinci by using instruments that he or she guides via a console.

The Da Vinci system translates your surgeon's hand movements at th console in real time, bending and rotating the instruments whil performing the procedure. The tiny wristed instruments move like human hand, but with a greater range of motion. The Da Vinci visio system also delivers highly magnified, 3D high-definition views of th surgical area. The instrument size makes it possible for surgeons t operate through one of a few small incisions.

Source - https://www.davincisurgery.com/da-vinci-systems/about-da-vinci-systems

Augmenting robots generally enhance capabilities that a person already has or replace capabilities that a person has lost.

Help your patients regain mobility with Eko Health.

Every year, 55.9 million people suffer from acquired brain injury, 15 million suffer from stroke, up to 500,000 people suffer from SCI, and 2.8 million people live with MS. Many of these people are left with limited mobility or some form of paralysis. This can be a devastating diagnosis that is completely life-changing for both patients and their families. Ekso Bionics addresses this by using our unique blend of clinical and engineering expertise to develop disruptive robotics for rehabilitation centres. Now, patients post stroke, brain injury or spinal cord injury and those affected by MS are able to utilise Ekso's exoskeletons in therapy to regain basic movements or even the ability to walk again. The wearer may experience an increase in range of motion and activation of muscles they had difficulty with before.

This technology can have incredible benefits for these individuals and give them a sense of independence back.

Source - https://eksobionics.com/

Expert System

An expert system is a program that uses artificial intelligence technology to simulate the knowledge and judgement of humans. Expert systems usually include a subject-specific knowledge base and can have additional modules added to expand their capacities.

The data in the knowledge base is essentially added by humans who are experts in a particular domain. However, the software is used by non-experts to gain information. It is used in various medical diagnoses, accounting, coding, gaming, and more areas.

There are 5 Components of expert systems:

1. Knowledge Base
2. Inference Engine
3. Knowledge acquisition and learning module
4. User Interface
5. Explanation module

Knowledge Base: This represents facts and rules. It consists of knowledge in a particular domain as well as rules to solve a problem, procedures and intrinsic data relevant to the domain.

Inference Engine: The function of the inference engine is to fetch the relevant knowledge from the knowledge base, interpret it and to find a solution relevant to the user's problem. The inference engine acquires the rules from its knowledge base and applies them to the known facts to infer new facts. Inference engines can also include an explanation and debugging abilities.

Knowledge Acquisition and Learning Module: The function of this component is to allow the expert system to acquire more and more knowledge from various sources and store it in the knowledge base.

User Interface: This module makes it possible for a non-expert user to interact with the expert system and find a solution to the problem.

Explanation Module: This module helps the expert system to give the user an explanation about how the expert system reached a particular conclusion.

Expert System

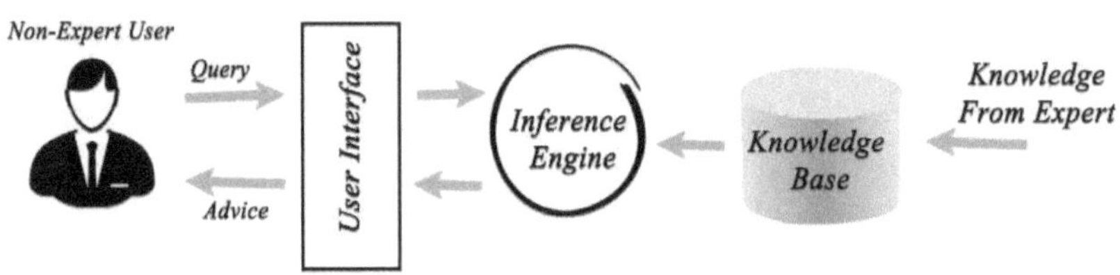

Example for Expert systems:

MYCIN : An early expert system, or artificial intelligence (AI) program, for treating blood infections. In 1972 work began on MYCIN at Stanford University in California. MYCIN would attempt to diagnose patients based on reported symptoms and medical test results. It can identify various bacteria that can cause severe infections and can also recommend drugs based on the person's weight.

DENDRAL: It is a program that analyses organic compounds to determine their structure. It is one of the early examples of a successful AI program and used for chemical analysis. It used a substance's spectrographic data to predict its molecular structure.

R1/XCON: This ES had the ability to select specific software to generate a computer system as per user preference.

PXDES: This system could easily determine the type and the degree of lung cancer in patients based on limited data.

CaDet: This clinical support system identifies cancer in its early stages.

DXplain: This is also a clinical support system that is capable of suggesting a variety of diseases based on just the findings of the doctor.

Different types of expert systems:

1. Rule-based systems
2. Frame-based systems
3. Hybrid systems
4. Model-based systems
5. Off the shelf systems
6. Custom made systems

Fuzzy Logic

According to Artificial Intelligence, Fuzzy Logic representation of scenarios where input data is unclear. In real time scenarios, there are not always clear answers to questions due to uncertainty. For example, if your wife asks you for next month's vacation plan, you might not have confidence and can not say "Yes" or "No". It is due to unknown circumstances that may arise in a month.

Computers mainly deal with boolean logic 1 or 0, 1 stands for true and 0 stands for false, but a fuzzy logic algorithm makes the system more intelligent and helps to understand the problem where there may be other answers than true or false.

Fuzzy logic was invented by Lotfi Zadeh in 1965, who observed that unlike computers, humans have a different range of possibilities between YES and NO, such as:

- Definitely yes
- Possibly yes
- Can't say
- Possibly no
- Definitely no

Let's take an example.

Question : Is it Cold today ?

Boolean answers -
- Yes
- No

Fuzzy Logic
- Very Cold
- Little Cold
- Moderate Cold
- Not at all

Fuzzy logic handles a question much better with multiple options to questions.

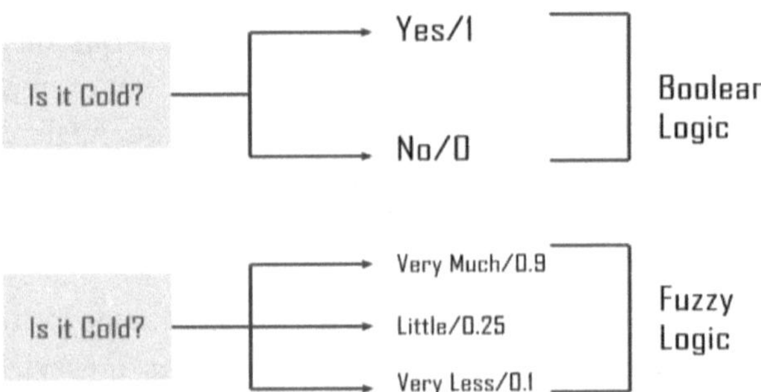

Different types of fuzzifier:

1. Singleton fuzzifier
2. Gaussian fuzzifier
3. Trapezoidal or triangular fuzzifier

Use cases

The Fuzzy Logic can be used in a variety of industries, including domestic goods, automotive systems, environment control, etc. Some of them are:

- It is used to control the altitude of aircraft, satellites, and spaceships.

- It is used in automotive systems to monitor and control the traffic and speed.

- The chemical industry uses Fuzzy Logic for processes like controlling the pH.

- Fuzzy Logic, coupled with technologies like Natural language processing and Artificial Intelligence, can enhance the capabilities of systems.

- It is extensively used in systems to automate vehicle control.

- The purpose of using Fuzzy Logic is to make decisions like a human in case of unclear data, but faster. Thus, making it suitable for Neural Networks.

Natural language processing

Natural language processing is a branch of artificial intelligence that helps computers understand, interpret and manipulate human language.

Natural language processing draws from many disciplines including computer science and computational linguistics in its pursuit to fill the gap between human communication and computer understanding.

Different types of Natural language processing (NLP)

1. Speech recognition
2. Machine translation

3. Natural language Inference
4. Sentiment analysis
5. Semantic search
6. Text Summarization
7. Text Classification

Speech Recognition

Speech recognition is the process of training machines to recognize spoken words and convert them into text. Research in this domain began at Bell Labs in the 1950s, when the world was introduced to the automatic digit recognition machine (named "Audrey"), which could recognize a human saying any number from zero to nine. Speech recognition has come a long way since then and in the last decade has benefited tremendously from deep learning techniques and the availability of rich speech recognition datasets.

Sound Hound

Sound Hound Inc. is an audio and speech recognition company founded in 2005. It develops speech recognition, natural language understanding, sound recognition and search technologies.

Brands can work with Sound Hound to develop and customise smart assistants using the company's voice AI platform. Netflix, Pandora and Mercedes-Benz are among the companies that have worked with Sound Hound on voice-enabled solutions. Building off its speech-to-meaning and deep meaning understanding technology, Sound Hound can integrate speech recognition, conversational AI and other components into cars and smart home devices.

Machine Translations

Machine translation examines how AI software can translate languages. In domains where fluency in multiple languages is required, machine translation can be extremely impactful. The European Union, for example, is required to translate all its cross-national policy documents into the 24 languages of its member states. Using machine translators can save time, improve efficiency, and lead to more consistent outcomes. Since 2017, neural networks have taken over machine translation. Unlike their predecessors, neural translators learn from a series of prior translation tasks and predict the likelihood of a sequence of words. Neural translation models have revolutionised the field of machine translation not only because they do not require human supervision, but also because they produce the most accurate translations. As a result, they have been widely deployed by search engines and social networks.

Natural Language Inference

Natural language inference is the task of determining whether, given a premise, a hypothesis is true (entailment), false (contradiction), or undetermined (neutral). This skill is also known as textual entailment as it requires determining whether a particular premise logically entails a hypothesis. Natural language inference necessitates language processing skills, such as named entity recognition (understanding the words you see), as well as being able to use common sense knowledge to distinguish between reasonable and unreasonable inferences.

Stanford Natural Language Inference (SNLI) The Stanford Natural Language Inference (SNLI) dataset contains around 600,000 sentence pairs (premise and associated hypothesis) that are labelled as either entailment, contradiction, or neutral. As part of this challenge, AI systems are asked whether premises logically entail certain hypotheses. Performance on SNLI is measured in accuracy based on the percentage of questions answered correctly.

	A senior is waiting at the window of a restaurant that serves sandwiches.	Relationship
P[a]	A person waits to be served his food.	Entailment
H[b]	A man is looking to order a grilled cheese sandwich.	Neutral
	A man is waiting in line for the bus.	Contradiction
[a]P, Premise.		
[b]H, Hypothesis.		

Sentimental Analysis

Sentiment analysis is the task of using NLP techniques to identify the sentiment (very negative, negative, neutral, positive, very positive) of a given text. Sentiment analysis can be straightforward if sentences are worded clearly and unambiguously, such as "I dislike winter weather." However, sentiment analysis can become more challenging when AI systems encounter sentences with flipped structures or negations, such as "to say that disliking winter weather is not really my thing is completely inaccurate."

Sentiment analysis has many commercial use cases, from parsing customer reviews and field survey responses to identifying the emotional states of customers.

Semantic Search

Natural Language Processing (NLP) has enabled a new paradigm of search and offers the power to massively improve our search experience. In short, NLP will improve search accuracy. Semantics is a branch of linguistics studying the meanings of words, their symbolic use, also including their multiple meanings.

Semantic search is search with meaning. This "meaning" can refer to various parts of the search process:

- understanding the query, instead of simply finding literal matches,
- or representing knowledge in a way suitable for meaningful retrieval.

Text Summarization

Text summarisation is the challenge of synthesising a piece of text while capturing its core content. Summarising texts is an important component of text classification, reading comprehension, and information dissemination; however, when done manually by humans, it is time- and labour-intensive. Developing AI systems that can functionally summarise texts has a number of practical use cases, from aiding universities in classifying academic papers to helping lawyers generate case summaries. Progress in text summarisation is often scored on ROUGE (Recall-Oriented Understudy for Gisting Evaluation). ROUGE calculates the overlap between a summary produced by an AI system and the reference summary produced by a human. The higher the ROUGE score, the greater the overlap and the more accurate the summary.

Text Classification

Text classification is a machine Learning approach for automatically categorising open-ended text into a number of predetermined categories. Text classifiers can structure, arrange, and classify almost any type of text, including articles, medical research, and customer tickets, as well as text found on the internet.

The traditional way of processing this data is to do it manually. However, this takes up a large portion of employees' time and can be very expensive.

Here's where automated text classification tools come to the rescue. They combine NLP and Machine Learning to structure and analyse enormous amounts of text in a time-saving and sustainable way.

This means that you can classify articles based on their topics, or organise support requests according to the problem they're trying to tackle. You could also evaluate your brand sentiment by analysing the tone of social media posts talking about your brand.

For example, if someone has tweeted: "The product is very user-friendly and simple," the text analysis tool could recognize user-friendly and simple, and assign them as relevant positive tags.

Use cases

- Email filter
- Smart assistants
- Search results
- Predictive text
- Language translation
- Digital phone calls
- Text analytics

Computer vision

Computer vision is one of the hottest subfields of artificial intelligence and machine learning given its wide variety of applications and tremendous potential. It's a goal to replicate the powerful capacities of human vision.

Computer vision system must recognize the present objects and their characteristics such as shapes, textures, colours, sizes, spatial arrangement, among other things to provide a description as complete as possible of the image.

Different techniques of computer vision:

1. Image classification
2. Image generation
3. Human Pose Estimation
4. Deep Face Detection

5. Semantic segmentation
6. Medical Image Segmentation
7. Face Detection and Recognition
8. Activity Recognition
9. Object detection
10. Visual Common-sense Reasoning (VCR)

Image Classification

Image classification refers to the ability of machines to categorise what they see in images and identify the 'class' the image falls under. (Or a probability of the image being part of a 'class'.) A class is essentially a label, for instance, 'car', 'animal', 'building' and so on.

The task of identifying what an image represents is called image classification. An image classification model is trained to recognize various classes of images. For example, you may train a model to recognize photos representing three different types of animals: rabbits, hamsters, and dogs.

Image Generation

Image generation (synthesis) is the task of generating new images from an existing dataset. Image generation is the task of generating images that are indistinguishable from real ones. Image generation can be widely useful in generative domains where visual content has to be created, for example, entertainment (companies like NVIDIA have already used image generators to create virtual worlds for gaming), fashion (designers can let AI systems generate different design patterns), and healthcare (image generators can synthetically create novel drug compounds). Figure 2.1.4 illustrates progress made in image generation by presenting several human faces that were synthetically generated by AI systems in the last year.

Human Pose Estimation

Human pose estimation is the task of estimating different positions of human body joints (arms, head, torso, etc.) from a single image (Figure 2.1.9), and then combining these estimates to correctly label the pose the human is taking. Human pose estimation can be used to facilitate activity recognition for purposes such as sports analytics, crowd surveillance, CGI development, virtual environment design, and transportation (for example, identifying the body language signs of an airport runway controller).

Deepfake Detection

Many AI systems can now generate fake images that are indistinguishable from real ones. A related technology involves superimposing one person's face onto another, creating a so-called "deepfake". Deepfakes are used for purposes ranging from advertising to generating misogynistic pornography and disinformation (in 2018, for example, a deep fake video of Barack Obama uttering profanities about Donald Trump was circulated online over 2 million times). In the last few years, AI researchers have sought to keep up with improving deep fake technologies by crafting stronger deep face detection algorithms.

Semantic Segmentation

Semantic segmentation is the task of assigning individual image pixels a category (such as person, bicycle, or background). A plethora of real world domains require pixel-level image segmentation such as autonomous driving (identifying which parts of the image a car sees are pedestrians and which parts are roads), image analysis (distinguishing the foreground and background in photos), and medical diagnosis (segmenting tumours in lungs).

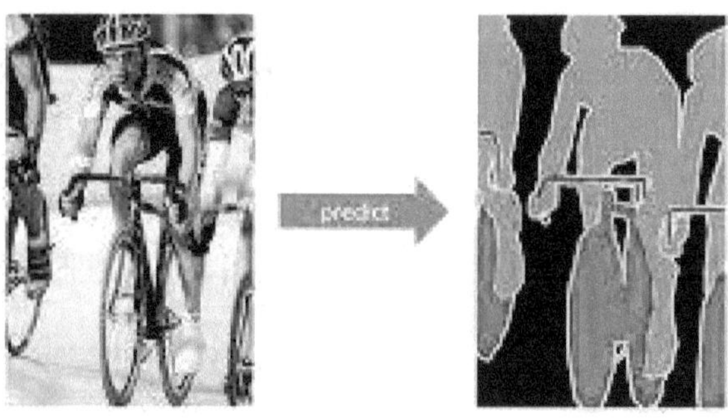

Medical Image Segmentation

Medical image segmentation refers to the ability of AI systems to segment objects of interest, such as organs, lesions, or tumours, in medical images. Technical progress in this task is vital to streamlining medical diagnoses. Advances in medical image segmentation mean doctors can spend less time on diagnosis and more time treating patients.

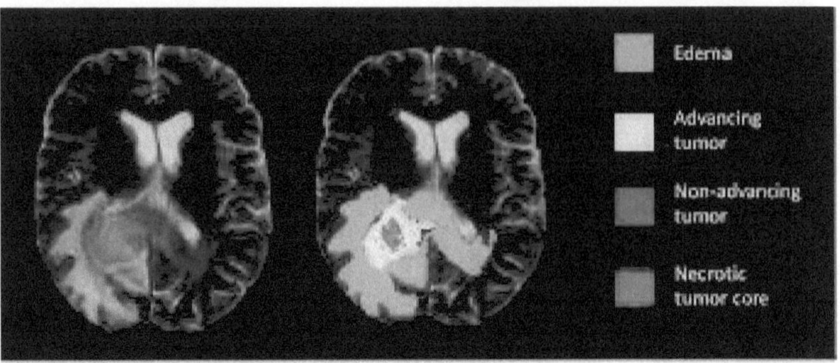

PathAI

PathAI's mission is to improve patient outcomes with AI-powered pathology. The PathAI platform promises substantial improvements to the accuracy of diagnosis and the efficacy of treatment of diseases like cancer, leveraging modern approaches in machine learning.

The company's machine learning algorithms help pathologists analyse tissue samples and make more accurate diagnoses.

PathAI has worked with the Bill & Melinda Gates Foundation and Philips to develop high-volume prognostic test support tools and plans for sustainable access to their advanced diagnostic services.

Face Detection and Recognition

In facial detection, AI systems are tasked with identifying individuals in images or videos. Although facial recognition technology has existed for several decades, the technical progress in the last few years has been significant. Some of today's top-performing facial recognition algorithms have a near 100% success rate on challenging datasets. Facial recognition can be used in transportation to facilitate cross-border travel, in fraud prevention to protect sensitive documents, and in online proctoring to identify illicit examination behaviour. The greatest practical promise of facial recognition, however, is in its potential to aid security, which makes the technology extremely appealing to militaries and governments all over the world (e.g., 18 out of 24 U.S. government agencies are already using some kind of facial recognition technology).

Activity Recognition

A fundamental subtask in video computer vision is activity recognition: identifying the activities that occur in videos. AI systems have been challenged to classify activities that range from simple actions, like walking, waving, or standing, to ones that are more complex and contain multiple steps, like preparing a salad (which requires an AI system to recognize and chain together discrete actions like cutting tomatoes, washing the greens, applying dressing, etc).

Object Detection

Object detection is the task of identifying objects within an image (Figure 2.2.4). There are different philosophies bearing on priority, speed, and accuracy that guide the design of object detection systems. Systems that train quickly might be more efficient but are less accurate. Those that are more accurate might perform better but take longer to process a video. This tradeoff between speed and accuracy is also reflected in the types of object detection methods pioneered in the last decade. There are one-stage methods which prioritise speed, such as SSD, RetinaNet, and YOLO, and two-stage methods which prioritise accuracy, such as Mask R-CNN, Faster R-CNN, and Cascade R-CNN.

Visual Common-sense Reasoning (VCR)

The Visual Common-sense Reasoning challenge is a relatively new benchmark for visual understanding. VCR asks AI systems to answer challenging questions about scenarios presented from images, and also to provide the reasoning behind their answers (unlike the VQA challenge, which only requires an answer). The dataset contains 290,000 pairs of multiple-choice questions, answers, and rationales from 110,000 image scenarios taken from movies. Figure 2.2.7 illustrates the kinds of questions posed in the VCR.

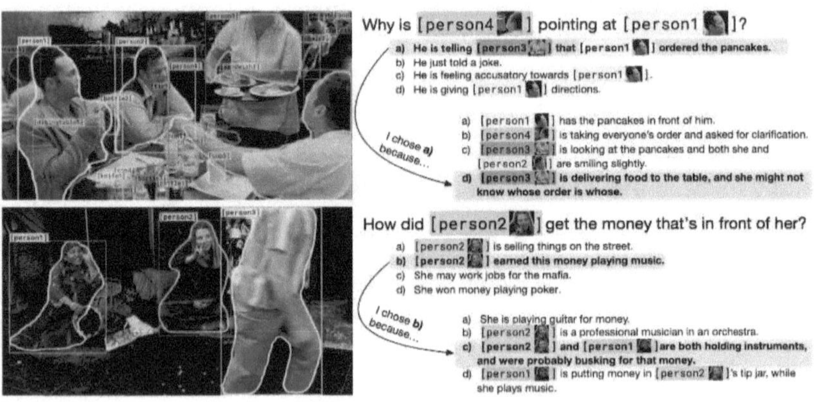

Summary

In this chapter, a brief introduction to Artificial Intelligence is outlined. The discussion included the basic concepts of AI, its different types of AI and stages. It also addresses different AI domains that includes machine learning concepts, natural language processing, computer vision, fuzzy logic and expert systems. We discussed basic concepts and real time implementation of different AL and other domain implementations.

- Machine learning is a subset of artificial intelligence. Machine learning focuses on the development of computer programs. Machine learning supports:
    - Supervised learning
    - Unsupervised learning
    - Reinforcement learning

- Deep Learning is an artificial intelligence (AI) function that imitates the working of the human brain in processing data and creating patterns for use in decision making.

- Robotics is a branch of engineering that involves the conception, design, manufacture, and operation of robots.

- An expert system is a program that uses artificial intelligence technology to simulate the knowledge and judgement of humans.

- Natural language processing is a branch of artificial intelligence that helps computers understand, interpret and manipulate human language.

- Computer vision system must recognize the present objects and their characteristics such as shapes, textures, colours, sizes, spatial arrangement, among other things to provide a description as complete as possible of the image.

References

- https://theconversation.com/understanding-the-four-types-of-ai-from-reactive-robots-to-self-aware-beings-67616
- https://builtin.com/artificial-intelligence
- https://aethon.com/mobile-robots-for-healthcare/
- https://blog.robotiq.com/teleoperated-robots-the-industrial-future-using-ar-and-vr
- https://www.davincisurgery.com/da-vinci-systems/about-da-vinci-systems
- https://eksobionics.com/
- https://www.professional-ai.com/rule-based-systems.html
- https://theconversation.com/understanding-the-four-types-of-ai-from-reactive-robots-to-self-aware-beings-67616
- https://builtin.com/artificial-intelligence
- https://www.raconteur.net/infographics/a-day-in-the-life-of-ai/
- https://somenplus.blogspot.com/2020/11/different-domains-of-artificial.html
- https://mind.ilstu.edu/curriculum/medical_robotics/prepro.html
- https://blog.robotiq.com/teleoperated-robots-the-industrial-future-using-ar-and-vr
- https://www.globaltechcouncil.org/artificial-intelligence/fuzzy-logic-what-it-is-and-some-real-life-applications/
- https://www.edureka.co/blog/fuzzy-logic-ai/
- https://towardsdatascience.com/semantic-search-73fa1177548f
- https://levity.ai/blog/text-classification
- https://datagovernance.com/quotes/data-quotes/

Seven

Think big with Big Data

Data is the new science. Big Data holds the answers. Are you asking the right questions?

-Pat Gelsinger, EMC

Introduction

This chapter provides a big data overview. Rather than elaborating on concrete individual technologies, this chapter provides a broad overview of big data concepts and technologies so that you may get a high-level understanding about the big data capabilities and individual technologies.

The concept of big data has been around for years. Organisation understands the importance of data and its impact on business. Now, it's an era where data is considered real assets or organisations. Most organisations understand that if they capture all the data stream into their business and apply suitable analytics, they can get significant value from it. Big data and analytics helps organisations harness their data and use it to identify new opportunities.

Let's understand big data and its values.

What is Big Data ?

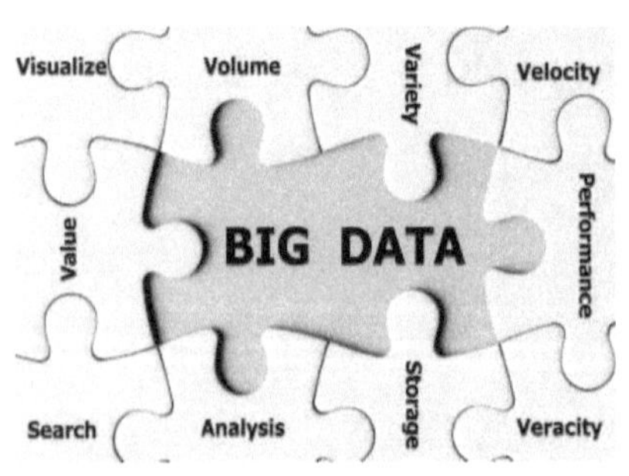

Big data refers to massive, complex data sets (either structured, semi-structured or unstructured) that are rapidly generated and transmitted from a wide variety of sources.

As discussed in the section "A Day in the Life of Data" data is constantly generated anytime we open an app or do any activities including search in google or simply travel from one place to another. Massive amount of data is generated and captured, managed, stored, analysed and visualised by the organisation.

Some example of big data:

- Facebook users shared 240K photos in a mint

- The New York Stock Exchange generates about one terabyte of new trade data per day.

- A single jet engine can generate 10+terabytes of data in 30 minutes of flight time. With many thousand flights per day, generation of data reaches up to many Petabytes.

Characteristics of Big Data

Early Big Data spans three dimensions: Volume, Velocity and Variety. As more organisation start to leverage the potential of big data, the list of "V's" has expanded:

Volume: Organisations collect data from a variety of sources, including transactions, smart (IoT) devices, industrial equipment, videos, images, audio, social media and more. In the past, storing all that data would have been too costly – but cheaper storage using data lakes, Hadoop and the cloud have eased the burden. According to articles "Data never Sleep" Google generates 5.7 M searches, Twitter with 575K tweets every second etc. With increase in mobile and IoT devices it is predicted that in the next few years data reach would be zettabytes per day.

Velocity: Data is generated at an ever-accelerating pace. Facebook users upload 44M views and 204K photos every second. The challenge for organisations is to find ways to collect, process, and make use of huge amounts of data as it comes in. With the enormous amount of data growth streams into businesses at an unprecedented speed and it is a challenge to handle in a timely manner. Specially in IoT cases, where sensors need to update information in near-real time.

Variety: Data comes in all types of formats – from structured, numeric data in traditional databases to unstructured text documents, emails, videos, audios, stock ticker data and financial transactions. Roughly 80 to 90 percent of all data is unstructured, meaning it is not easy to fit into a traditional database model.

Veracity: This refers to the quality of data, data comes from so many different sources, it's difficult to link, match, cleanse and transform data across systems.

Variability: Data flows are unpredictable – changing often and varying greatly. It's challenging, but businesses need to know when something is trending in social media, and how to manage daily, seasonal and event-triggered peak data loads.

Viscosity: Refers to how difficult the data is to use or integrate.

How UPS - leverage Big Data

About UPS (United Parcels Services) :

UPS is an American multinational package delivery and supply chain management organisation founded in 1907. The company offers forwarding and logistics services across the globe. UPS is a global leader in logistics, offering a broad range of solutions including the transportation of packages and freight, the facilitation of international trade, and the deployment of advanced technology to manage the world of business more efficiently.

Challenges

In his interview Dave Barnes, CTO of UPS , company wanted to solve wad Route Optimization, according to Dave, a saving a mile in a day per driver could result in a saving of 1.5 million gallons of fuel per year, which equals $ 50 million in savings annually.

Average stop for a driver was 120 to 140 per day, it lists down to a huge possible permutation combination of data and normal humans can not think. UPS generates a huge volume of data per day with different varieties and velocity. The data was spreaded in different data sources, RDBMS, spreadsheet, local repository

Solution

Big data handles five "V" of data effectively, Volume, Velocity, Variety, Veracity and Variability. With the help of the big data ecosystem, UPS developed ORION (On-Road Integrated Optimisation and Navigation)

that leveraged the storage and computing capacity. ORION uses fleet telematics and advanced algorithms to take route optimisation to the next level. ORION is capable of delivering tens of thousands route optimizations per minute based on real-time information. ORION not only helped UPS on route optimisation but extending the application in the field of predictive and prescriptive analytics as well

Source - https://datafloq.com/read/ups-spends-1-billion-big-data-annually/

Benefit of Big Data

Everyone is talking about big data trends. Industries are looking at the big data ecosystem as a game changer and with the ecosystem organisations harness their data and use it to identify new opportunities. That, in turn, leads to smarter business moves, grab new opportunities, more efficient operations, higher profits, reduce customer churn rates, and happier customers. Businesses that use big data are looking to gain value in many ways such as.

5 Ways Walmart Uses Big Data to Help Customers

Big data is an essential part of strategy for many companies, and Walmart is analysing data in distinct ways.

To Make Walmart Pharmacies more efficient

Walmart uses simulations at the pharmacy to find out how many prescriptions are filled in a day and to determine a busiest time during a day or month. This data helps pharmacy staff scheduling and to reduce the amount of time it takes a prescription to be filled.

To Improve Store checkout

2

Walmart is testing how to use big data to improve store checkout experience. By using predictive analytics, stores can anticipate demand at certain hours and determine how many associates are needed at the counters. By analysing the data Walmart can determine the best form of checkout for each store: Self checkout or facilitated checkout.

To Manage the Steps of a Supply Chain

3

Walmart uses simulations to track the number of steps from the dock to the store. This allows the company to optimise the routes to the shipping dock and track the number of times a product gets touched along the way to the customer. The company uses the data to analyse transportation lanes and routes for the company's fleet of trucks. The data helps Walmart keep transportation costs down and schedule driver time.

To Optimise Product Assortment

4

Through analysis of customer preferences and shopping patterns, Walmart can accelerate decision making on how to stock store shelves and display merchandise. Big data provides insight on new items, discontinued products and which private brands to carry.

To Personalise Shopping Experience

5

Big data allows Walmart to identify a shopper's preferences to develop a consistent and delightful shopping experience. If a user is shopping for baby products, Walmart can use data analysis to personalise mobile deals for parents and help them live better by anticipating their needs.

Like Walmart example, big data helps businesses to accelerate their business with new opportunities and optimise your business solution. Big data could help

- Improve services and identify new opportunities
- Optimise operational cost and processes
- Helps you understand the customer behaviours
- Helps you for better decision-making process
- Helps customer retention
- Process Optimisation

Big Data Solution Stages

Any big data solution design includes 5 important stages.

- Big Data Ingestion
- Big Data Storage
- Big Data Analytics
- Big Data Visualisation
- Big Data Security

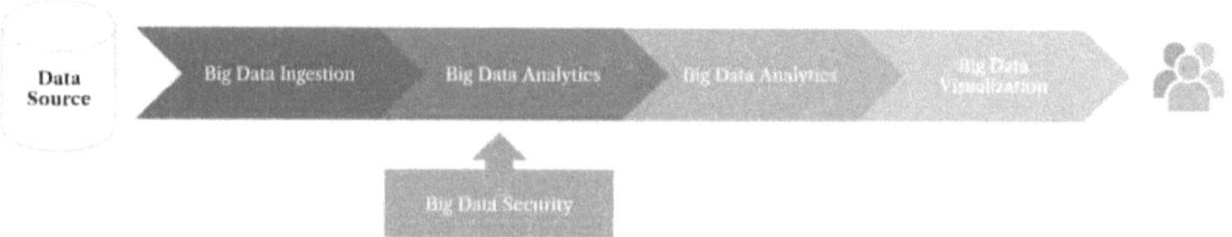

We will discuss more on each of the above topics in the following sections.

Big Data Ingestion

We have discussed the data pipeline in chapter Transfer and Transform your data. Big data ingestion is the sub-set of building a data pipeline. Big data ingestion gathers data and brings it into a data processing system where it can be stored, analysed and accessed. In short, the job of big data ingestion is collecting and storing both structured and unstructured data into a centralised location.

Depending upon business goal, and nature of source and destination data, data ingestion can be real time, batches or both (called Lambda architecture). Data at real time streaming is captured once it is emitted at the source side whereas in batch data is transferred at regular intervals from the source system.

In many situations, source and destination data format is different to make it usable and consistent, it is required to transform source data as per destination data requirement.

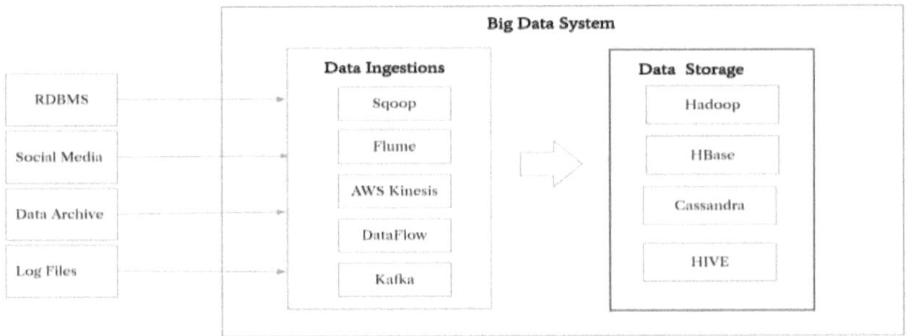

While selecting the right Big Data ingestion tools it is important to consider parameters like,
- velocity of data: The movement of data can be massive or continuous size.
- Frequency of data: Should could in real time or batch
- Format of data: Ingestion data can be in different formats (structured, unstructured, or semi structured)
- Size of data: Collecting data from multiple sources could increase data ingestion time.

Some commonly use Big Data Ingestions are:

Apache Sqoop: It is a part of the Hadoop ecosystem and a tool designed for efficiently transferring bulk data between Apache Hadoop and structured datastores such as relational databases. You can write Sqoop jobs using Sqoop scripts. Integrating Sqoop with Oozie allows for the scheduling and automating of import and export tasks. The Sqoop architecture is a connector-based architecture that can support plugins, which provides connectivity to new external sources.

Apache Flume: Apache Flume is a tool for data ingestion (Import/Export) mechanism for collecting, aggregating and transporting large amounts of streaming data such as log files, events (etc...) from various sources to a centralised data store. Flume is a highly reliable, distributed, and configurable tool. It is principally designed to copy streaming data (log data) from various web servers to HDFS.

Apache Kafka is an open-source distributed streaming system used for stream processing, real-time data pipelines, and data integration at scale. Originally created to handle real-time data feeds at LinkedIn in 2011. Kafka quickly evolved from messaging queue to a full-fledged event streaming platform capable of handling over 1 million messages per second, or trillions of messages per day.

Kafka provides three main functions to its users:
- Publish and subscribe to streams of records
- Effectively store streams of records in the order in which records were generated
- Process streams of records in real time

Apache Nifi: It is another of the best Ingestion tools that provide an easy-to-use, powerful, and reliable system to process and distribute information. Apache NiFi supports robust and scalable directed graphs of routing, transformation, and system mediation logic. Functions of Apache Nifi are: Track information flow from beginning to end.

Amazon Kinesis is a powerful and automated cloud-based service that empowers businesses to extract, and analyse real-time data streams. The platform can capture, process, and store both videos (via Kinesis Video Streams) and data streams (using Kinesis Data Streams).

Google Dataflow enables fast, simplified streaming data pipeline development with lower data latency.

Big Data Storage

This section will talk more about big data storage overview. We discussed big data characteristics, big data storage technologies should address the volume, velocity or varieties in some way. Big data storage is different from relational database storage. Relational databases can handle the challenges but big data needs some alternate approach in storing data like, column databases, distributed databases like Hadoop Distributed file systems (HDFS).

As we are talking about a huge volume of data, big data storage should address volume challenges by making use of distributed and shared nothing architecture. Architecture should support high availability with scaling out new nodes whenever it is required for computation and storage. Horizontal scaling with the help of commodity hardware is major game changers for enterprise. As storage is cheaper now, more and more companies are storing, managing and analysing their business data. NoSQL storage technologies are also a key enabler to efficiently analyse large amounts of data.

Different types of storage systems include

- **Distributed File System**: As the name suggests, is a file system that is distributed on multiple file servers or multiple locations. It allows programs to access or store isolated files as they do with the local ones, allowing programmers to access files from any network or computer. Hadoop File system (HDFS) provides a distributed file system that runs on commodity hardwares.

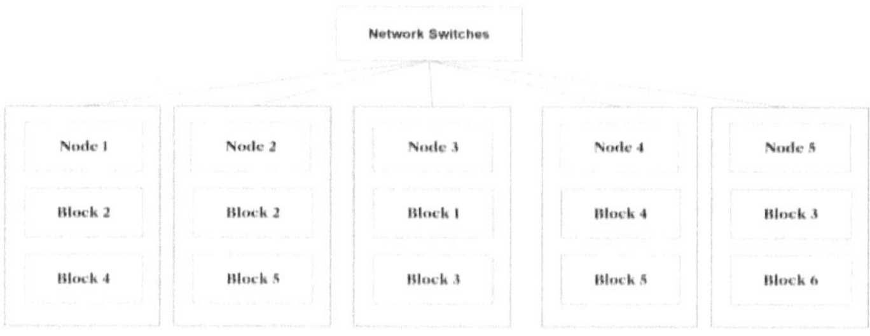

Commodity hardware is a mid-range server with less memory and mid-level hardware. Machine may have 32GB-96GB of RAM 2GHz processor. Machines are connected with network switches. Data is distributed across clusters of machines. Each piece of data is called a block. In order to prevent data loss blocks are redundant in multiple machines. If one machine fails, data is processed by another machine which has the same block.

Big data processing is a set of techniques or programming models to access large-scale data to extract useful information for supporting and providing decisions.

Distributed Processing: In distributed, data processing is divided into parallel tasks as many as the number of blocks. Tasks are distributed to the cluster of machines. Task is executed where data is instead of bringing data into the process.

For example, if a process needs to execute for Block 2 then send Task 1 to Node 1.

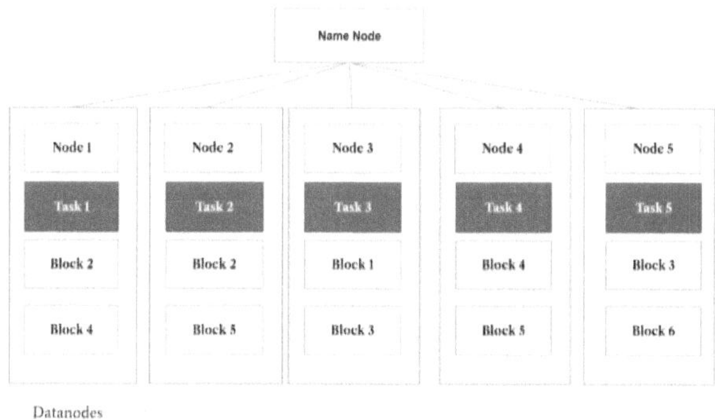

If node 1 fails then the same task will execute on node 2 for block 2.

- **NoSQL Database:** NoSQL databases enable a lot of opportunities in Big data areas, NoSQL is the most important storage in the big data family. NoSQL databases use models from outside relational databases. Some common NoSQL database models are

  - Key Value Store

  - Columnar Store

  - Document databases

  - Graph databases

- **Big Data Query:** Big data query facades on top of underlying big data store that simplifies data access process by supporting querying the underlying data store. They typically offer SQL like query interfaces for accessing data. A good example is HIVE provides abstraction on top of HDFS and executes queries by translating queries into MapReduce jobs. Spark SQL, PIG are other examples for scripting or SQL query enable tools.

- **Cloud Storage:** Maintaining big data storage at a data centre or own premises is not an easy task. Supporting high scalability with low latency is a real challenge with an on premises / data centre approach. The other method of storing massive amounts of data is cloud storage. The cloud provides not only readily available infrastructure but also the ability to scale this infrastructure quickly to manage large increases in traffic or usage.

  There are many cloud options available in markets but Amazon AWS, Microsoft Azure, Google GCP, IBM are post popular and preferable cloud options available and support Big Data solutions.

  - AWS - S3
  - Google Cloud Storage
  - Microsoft Blob Storage
  - IBM Cloud Object Storage

Big Data Analytics and Processing

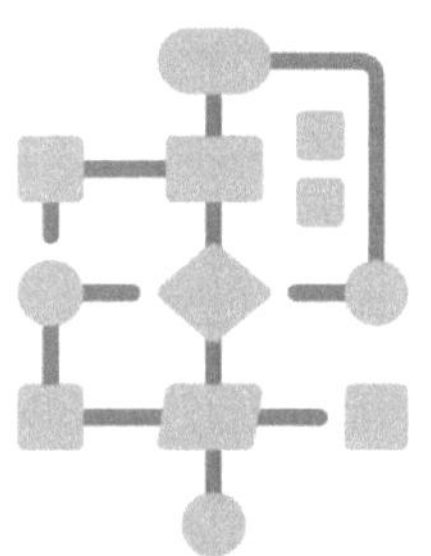 True value of big data is measured by the degree to which you are able to analyse and get something out of data. In this section, we will discuss what we can do with big data analytics. When we talk about big data analytics, it is about more than terabytes or petabytes of data. You can not analyse such huge data with a single server rather need multiple servers with distributed environments.

In order to successfully analyse, data must be first sorted, organised, cleaned and transformed by a series of applications or tools.

Big data analysis can be possible with the help of:

- **Data Mining**: Big data analytics get data insight from data through knowledge discovery processes like data mining. Different data mining techniques help to extract underlying data patterns, find correlation among data and find trends in both structured and unstructured data.
Classification, clustering, association rule and regression algorithms mainly used to get big data decisions.

- **Predictive Analytics:** Machine learning and other types of statistical algorithms help to build analytical models that predict customer pattern and behaviours. With the help of machine learning and AI models along with big data help to optimise processes, cost and services.

- **Real Time Analytics:** Using big data streaming pipeline solutions and algorithms it allows you to gain insight at real time.

Big Data Tools to support Analytics includes

MapReduce: Hadoop MapReduce is a software framework for easily writing applications which process vast amounts of data (multi-terabyte data-sets) in-parallel on large clusters (thousands of nodes) of commodity hardware in a reliable, fault-tolerant manner.

A MapReduce job usually splits the input data-set into independent chunks which are processed by the map tasks in a completely parallel manner. The framework sorts the outputs of the maps, which are then input to the reduced tasks. Typically both the input and the output of the job are stored in a file-system. The framework takes care of scheduling tasks, monitoring them and re-executes the failed tasks.

Apache Hive: It is an open source data warehouse software for reading, writing and managing large data set files that are stored directly in either the Apache Hadoop Distributed File System (HDFS) or other data storage systems such as Apache HBase. Hive enables SQL developers to write Hive Query Language (HQL) statements that are similar to standard SQL statements for data query and analysis. It is designed to make MapReduce programming easier because you don't have to know and write lengthy Java code. Instead, you can write queries more simply in HQL, and Hive can then create the map and reduce the functions.

Apache Pig: Apache Pig is an abstraction over MapReduce. It is a tool/platform which is used to analyse larger sets of data representing them as data flows. Pig is generally used with Hadoop; we can perform all the data manipulation operations in Hadoop using Pig. For writing data analysis programs, Pig renders a high-level programming language called Pig Latin. Several operators are provided by Pig Latin using which personalised functions for writing, reading, and processing of data can be developed by programmers.

Apache Spark: It is an open source data-processing engine for large data sets. It is designed to deliver the computational speed, scalability, and programmability required for big data—specifically for streaming data, graph data, machine learning, and artificial intelligence (AI) applications. Spark is designed to support a wide range of data analytics tasks, ranging from simple data loading and SQL queries to machine learning and streaming computation, over the same computing engine and with a consistent set of APIs.

Spark is often compared to Apache Hadoop, and specifically to MapReduce, Hadoop's native data-processing component. The chief difference between Spark and MapReduce is that spark processes and keeps the data in memory for subsequent steps—without writing to or reading from disk—which results in dramatically faster processing speeds.

Feature of Apache Spark

- **Speed** — Spark helps to run an application in Hadoop cluster, up to 100 times faster in memory, and 10 times faster when running on disk. This is possible by reducing the number of read/write operations to disk. It stores the intermediate processing data in memory.

- **Supports multiple languages** — Spark provides built-in APIs in Java, Scala, or Python. Therefore, you can write applications in different languages

- **Advanced Analytics**- Spark not only supports 'Map reduce', it supports SQL queries, streaming data, machine learning(ML).

Big Data Visualization

You have done analysis and are looking for the result. Visualisation helps to identify patterns in your data and the results. In this section, we will cover the visualisation aspect of big data. In the upcoming next chapter, we will cover in depth visualisation techniques. Data visualisations are a crucial component of data analysis, data science and big data analytics. Visual information processing aids data scientists and data analysts in

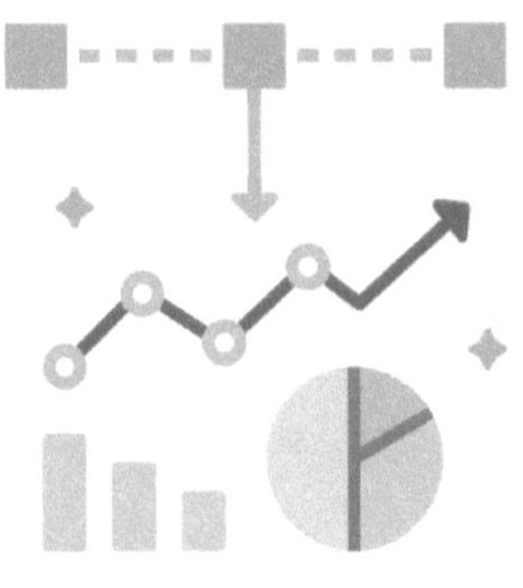

decision-making, exploration and discovery, communication, and in presenting data in a consumable format.

New tools for data visualisation that supports big data ecosystems includes:

Tableau: Tableau is data visualisation tools that are widely used for business intelligence. It helps to create interactive graphs, charts and dashboard to gain better business insight.

Apache Zeppelin: It is an open-source, web-based "notebook" that enables interactive data analytics and collaborative documents. The notebook is integrated with distributed, general-purpose data processing systems such as Apache Spark (large-scale data processing), Apache Flink (stream processing framework), and many others. Apache Zeppelin allows you to make beautiful, data-driven, interactive documents with SQL, Scala, R, or Python right in your browser.

Qlikview: Qlik offers a full range of interactive visualisations and robust AI support including association recommendations and data preparation.

R: R is a statistical programming tool and used for data analysis. In R you can create visually appealing data by writing a few lines of code.

Java Script charts: Some Java script libraries are widely used for data visualisation purposes that includes D3.js, High charts, AM Charts, Fusion charts etc.

Big Data Security

 Security is a constant threat as data is valuable assets for industry. Big Data Security is the collective term for all measures and tools used to guard both data and analytic methods from internal, external attacks, thefts or malicious activities that could cause data loss.

Safeguard Distributed Programming Framework:

Authentication and Access Control: Creates trust using methods like **Kerberos**, Kerberos is a network authentication protocol developed by the Massachusetts Institute of Technology (MIT). Kerberos Authentication and ensuring that predefined security policies are followed.

Kerberos is supported by hadoop and other big data tools for secure connection. Kerberos protocol uses secret-key cryptography to provide secure communications over a non-secure network. Primary benefits are strong encryption and single sign-on (SSO). It only allowed users to be given access.

The Apache Knox Gateway ("Knox") provides perimeter security so that the enterprise can confidently extend Hadoop access to more of those new users while also maintaining compliance with enterprise security policies. Knox also simplifies Hadoop security for users who access the cluster data and execute jobs.

Mandatory access control (MAC): It is a method of limiting access to resources based on the sensitivity of the information that the resource contains and the authorization of the user to access information with that level of sensitivity. MAC tools like **Apache Sentry** allow access to files based on a predefined security policy and ensure that untrusted code does not leak information through device resources.

Centralised Administration and Audit: Auditing is necessary for managing security compliance and other requirements like security forensics tools like Apache Ranger provides centralised security administration to manage all security related tasks. Apache Ranger is a framework to enable, monitor, and manage comprehensive data security across the Hadoop platform. Apache Ranger provides security across the Hadoop ecosystem and defines access for HDFS, Hive, YARN, HBASE, Storm etc.

Data at rest/in-motion Encryption: NoSQL database vulnerable to NoSQL injection attack. Data must be encrypted at rest and at motion using algorithms such as advanced encryption standard (AES), RSA, or Safe Hash Algorithm.

Big Data on Cloud

Big data is all about dealing with the massive scale of data, and data is growing day by day. Storing and processing such huge data with high scalability is a real challenge. Big data requires massive on-demand computation power and distributed storage. Cloud computing provides on demand computation and storage resources very seamlessly.

Cloud computing offers distributed processing for scalability and expansion through virtual machines. This would help to meet exponential data growth. Along with data storage, cloud provides computation capability. Computation of analytics over big data could be coupled or decoupled. Data storage with computation power has advantages on performance over decouple services which supports flexibility.

Cloud provides serverless capability, it is also becoming popular where you pay only for the amount of data processing and complexity of data and don't have to reserve computing resources.

Service providers like Amazon Web Services (AWS), Microsoft Azure and Google Cloud offer big data systems in a cost-efficient manner to capture data and analytical services.

Big Data on AWS:
Amazon AWS provides a wide variety of tools and services that supports big data ecosystems.

Amazon Redshift: Amazon Redshift is a data warehouse product which forms part of the larger cloud-computing platform Amazon Web Services. Redshift can easily run and scale analytics in seconds without provisioning and managing a data warehouse. Redshift processes petabytes of data with a fraction of costs.

Redshift Spectrum: You can use redshift spectrum along with Redshift cluster to query data in S3

S3: A data lake built on AWS uses Amazon S3 as its primary storage platform. Amazon S3 provides an optimal foundation for a data lake because of its virtually unlimited scalability and high durability. S3 provides a wide range of storage depending on the use cases e.g. S3 Glacier and S3 Deep Glacier for long-term archive and digital preservation with retrieval in hours at the lowest cost storage in the cloud.

AWS EMR: AWS also provides another very popular service Elastic Map Reduce (EMR) that provides Hadoop and Spark on demand. Which Hadoop ecosystem including Namenode, data node configurations. This EMR service provides Hadoop ecosystem within a click and all software readily available.

AWS Glue is a serverless data integration service that makes it easier to discover, prepare, move, and integrate data from multiple sources for analytics, machine learning (ML), and application development.

AWS Kinesis: With Amazon Kinesis, you can ingest real-time data such as video, audio, application logs, website clickstreams, and IoT telemetry data for machine learning, analytics, and other applications. Amazon Kinesis enables you to process and analyse data as it arrives and respond instantly instead of having to wait until all your data is collected before the processing can begin.

Big Data on Azure

Azure Data Lake Storage Gen 2: It is a set of capabilities dedicated to big data analytics, built on Azure Blob Storage. It is stores petabytes of data. Azure Data Lake Storage is capable of storing large quantities of structured, semi-structured, and unstructured data in their original file formats. For example, it can store Text files, CSV files, JSON files, XML files, images, videos, etc. When the uploading of files gets completed after that we can use open-source technologies like Databricks, or Hadoop, to process and analyse the data as per our business needs.

Azure HD Insight: Azure HDInsight is a cloud distribution of Hadoop components. Azure HDInsight makes it easy, fast, and cost-effective to process massive amounts of data in a customizable environment. You can use the most popular open-source frameworks such as Hadoop, Spark, Hive, LLAP, Kafka and more.

Azure SQL Database: Azure SQL database supports distributed SQL server. The Apache Spark connector for Azure SQL Database and SQL Server enables these databases to act as input data sources and output data sinks for Apache Spark jobs. It allows you to use real-time transactional data in big data analytics and persist results for ad-hoc queries or reporting.

Azure Stream Analytics: Is serverless real time analytics. Azure Stream Analytics is a fully managed, real-time analytics service designed to help you analyse and process fast moving streams of data that can be used to get insights, build reports or trigger alerts and actions. Learn how to use Azure Stream Analytics with our quick starts, tutorials, and samples.

Azure Machine Learning Service: It is a cloud service for accelerating and managing the machine learning project lifecycle. Machine learning professionals, data scientists, and engineers can use it in their day-to-day workflows: Train and deploy models, and manage MLOps.

Big Data on Google Cloud

Big Query: The BigQuery service replaces the typical hardware setup for a conventional data warehouse. It is a fully-managed, serverless data warehouse that enables scalable analysis over petabytes of data. You don't need to provide the computer resources, you just need to provide the query and data, google bigquery decides the computation power to run the query.

Big Query ML: Allows you to create and execute machine learning models in Big Query using standard SQL queries. Big Query Machine Learning (BQML) is a toolset that allows you to train and serve machine learning models directly in Big Query

Dataproc: It is a managed Spark and Hadoop service that lets you take advantage of open source data tools for batch processing, querying, streaming, and machine learning. Dataproc automation helps you create clusters quickly, manage them easily, and save money by turning clusters off when you don't need them.

Pub/Sub and Dataflow: You can ingest and store real-time data directly into cloud storage, scaling both in and out in response to data volume. Dataflow use for data transformation in analytical pipeline.

Challenges with Big Data

Data Volume: Data today is growing at an exponential rate. Current big data ecosystem might not be sufficient to handle multifold growth of such huge data and useful for analysis.

Storage: Cloud computing is helping to manage infrastructure effortlessly and cost effectively for big data but this complicates the decision to host big data solutions outside the enterprise.

Data retention: How long should one retain this data? Data purging and archiving data is important, some data may require for long-term decision, but some data may quickly become irrelevant and obsolete.

Skilled professionals: Skill In order to develop, manage and run those applications that generate insights, organisations need professionals who possess a high-level proficiency in data sciences.

Big Data At Caesars Entertainment

Background

Caesars Entertainment, formerly known as Harrah's – the company which runs the famous Caesar's Palace Las Vegas and more than 50 other casinos worldwide. They were facing bankruptcy and had been hit with a $1.5 million fine over irregularities in their accounts.

Challenges

The US casino industry has been in decline for many years, in terms of money spent at the gaming tables. This isn't necessarily a problem if you own a large hotel and gambling facility, though – because at the same time the luxury hospitality sector has been booming. Middle classes have emerged among the developing
world's populations, hungry for a taste of international travel and Western-style indulgence.

Solution

Gary Loveman introduced Caesars Total Rewards scheme.Caesar's loyalty program, Total Rewards, earned the company a reputation as a big data pioneer on the Vegas strip. The program was launched in 1998 with some intuition made by casino operation and science base analytical tools. Like most other rewards/loyalty programs, the casino's program allows customers to "advance" through reward tiers as they spend more. As they spend with the rewards card, customers are rewarded with meals, room upgrades, show tickets, limo rides – all the way up to complimentary stays, flights for top tier members. The membership card is used at almost every point of contact within the casino chain, and each contact offers another point of data.

In exchange, Caesar receives a plethora of information on the customer and his/her behaviour while in the casino. Data mining has led Caesar's to develop 90 different customer segment classifications, each of which responds differently to different marketing approaches – again allowing for a more customer-centric approach to service.

With data being captured from the moment the trip is booked online, each individual customer's trip is monitored in real time (often times including location data from customers using the mobile app) – shopping behaviour, meals purchased, etc. – information which allows for the casino to react much faster, deliver a best-in-class customer experience, and, ultimately, lead the customer to spend even more money. All offers and transactions are continually calculating/recalculating a customer's lifetime value to the casino and all decisions made by representatives are linked back to this valuable metric.

Due to the data-drive strategy, a remarkable achievement and in addition it has given Caesars unique insights into the behaviour of their customers. As Joshua Kanter, vice president of Total Rewards for Caesars Entertainment, Las Vegas, says: Big Data is even more important than a gaming licence.

Summary

In this chapter, an attempt is made to summarise big data processes. The chapter begins with the fundamental concepts of big data and different big data characteristics. Also we discuss different stages of big data that includes big data ingestion, data storage, big data analytics and big data security. The chapter provides a basic overview of each stage and tool techniques used in each stage.

Chapter also covers benefits of big data and its impact on business with the help of Walmart and Caesars Entertainment examples.

References

- https://www.researchgate.net/publication/299617100_Big_Data_Storage
- https://scalegrid.io/blog/data-visualization-using-apache-zeppelin/
- https://datafloq.com/read/for-caesars-entertainment-big-data-is-more-importa/
- https://digital.hbs.edu/platform-digit/submission/caesars-entertainment-what-happens-in-vegas-ends-up-in-a-1billion-database/

Eight

Dress up your data with charts and graphs

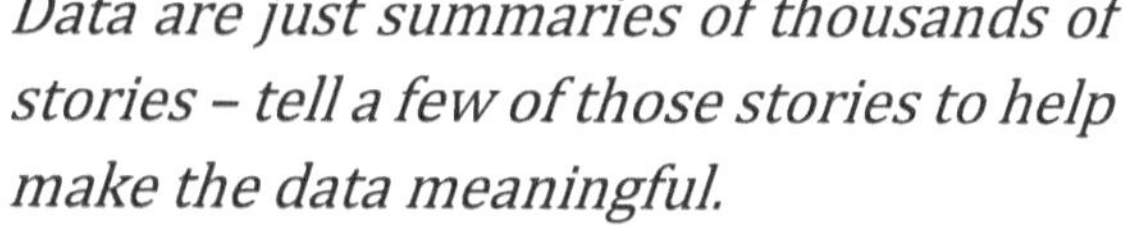

Data are just summaries of thousands of stories – tell a few of those stories to help make the data meaningful.

– Chip & Dan Heath, Authors of Made to Stick, Switch

Introduction

Human brain processes data quicker and more efficiently when data is in graphical form. To understand how we are able to interpret data visualisations so effectively, it is important to understand how our brain perceives and processes information. In this chapter, you will learn how different charts, images and visualisation techniques tell you data stories. Data visualisation means drawing graphic displays to show data. Data visualisations use distinctive techniques and design to guide users to easily absorb, understand, and make decisions based on information. Data visualisation enhances learning, understanding, and reasoning and helps the stakeholders to make effective and fast decision making. It also provides a better understanding for pattern recognition, analysis of trends, and to extract the appropriate information from the visuals.

Important of Visualisation

Let's consider an example, the below table contains 12 months sales data for four regions (East, West, North and South). Take a look at the numbers.

What are trend sales for Years 2021 ?

Regions	North	South	East	West
Jan	$7.2K	$6.3K	$5.3K	$6.1K
Feb	$6.4K	$6.7K	$5.8K	$6.1K
March	$8.1K	$7.1K	$6.9K	$6.2K
April	$9.5K	$7.4K	$7.2K	$6.2K
June	$6.8K	$7.6K	$7.4K	$6.3K
July	$7.4K	$7.7K	$7.5K	$6.4K
August	$7.9K	$8.1K	$7.7K	$6.4K
Sept	$8.2K	$8.4K	$7.8K	$6.4K
Oct	$6.5K	$7.6K	$8.1K	$6.4K
Nov	$6.9K	$7.4K	$9.3K	$6.5K
Dec	$8.1K	$7.3K	$8.4K	$6.5K

What you can see? Are any trends or patterns in data easily identified? I guess you can figure out the pattern with some additional effort, but it's possible. Let's assume you have an enormous amount of data then what do you think?

Now let's represent the same data in a better way.

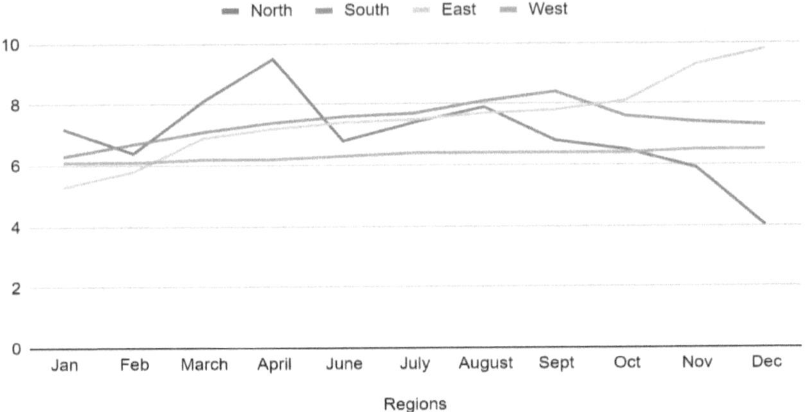

Using simple visualisation techniques you can simply identify trends and spot relationships. You can easily identify that the north region has lower sales trends and the trend is decreasing significantly whereas East region sales have upward moves.

With the help of visual trends, one can easily understand what can be the best next step. It makes the data less confusing and more shareable and accessible.

With the above example, you might get an idea of how data visualisation would benefit. Data visualisation is essential to assist businesses in quickly identifying data trends, which would otherwise be a hassle. Here are some more benefits:

- **Information easier to understand**

  Enormous amounts of data are generated every day, It is impossible to absorb all that information looking at the raw data. The human brain can process visual cues faster than numeric or text data. Visual impressions stay longer in mind than others. Data visualisation techniques help to simplify complex data information that is easy to understand.

- **Better Business Analysis**

Business generates valuable information everyday. It's important to understand data and take the right actions. This information is crucial because it can show profits, losses, and return on investment. This helps you to see where you can maximise your profits, remain relevant in your industry, and meet your customer needs. Data visualisation connects all crucial data points and gives everybody valuable insight into how different data sets are connected to each other. A visual representation of data helps companies increase their profits through better analysis and better business decisions.

- **Fast decision-making**

Visualisation makes data transparent so that decision-makers can comprehend and make decisions faster. The real-time data helps them make decisions that significantly impact the organisation. For example, the data can help sales managers to see where the sales team should concentrate to close sales more quickly.

- **Save Valuable Time**

You can imagine the pain if you need to figure out a data pattern by scanning millions of records without any data visualisation tools. You would have to dedicate a lot of time to scan through the raw data and extract information for reports. Data visualisation tools and techniques make it easy for us and save our valuable time.

Pre-attentive Attributes

Pre-attentive attributes are visual properties that we notice without using conscious effort to do so. Pre-attentive processes take place within 200 ms after exposure to a visual stimulus, and do not require sequential search.

In the book "Information Visualisation: Perception for Design", Colin Ware presents four categories of pre-attentive visual properties:

- Form
- Colour
- Movement
- Special Positioning

Let's take a real-life example

Where do your eyes go?

If your answer is you are not sure, or have no idea then you are right. All the fruits and vegetables in the image are very common and equally highlighted.

Where are your eyes naturally drawn ?

This time you might notice that your eyes were immediately drawn towards the red boat. Your iconic memory stimulus in the environment is noticeably different from its surrounding. It will be easy to keep their attention exactly where you would like it.

Now apply the same real-time concepts in the business world, look at the figure below How many 4s are there? What would be your general approach, scans entire data and counts 4s, it is a time-consuming process and high chance of getting errors.

```
8652746976135176863930376123
3239868326592124699292229021
9278383766982322211784099967
2489238989867232637855900018
5789129649893221972410552216
4989430293015430358201455637
1432987876543917034709150212
0765896213740098843265701230
3278912469925783012638909180
```

What would be an easy way? Simply colour difference. It is easy to find one blue 4s on a table of hundreds of digits. Our eyes and brain are amazing at spotting such highlighted things very easily and effectively.

Pre-attentive attributes

There are many pre-attentive attributes, some of them are:

- Forms
- Colours
- Special Positioning
- Motions

Form

Form itself sub-categorised into many sub attributes like length, shape, width, size, curvature, orientation, spatial grouping, added mark, enclosure etc. Size and length are mostly used among other sub categories.

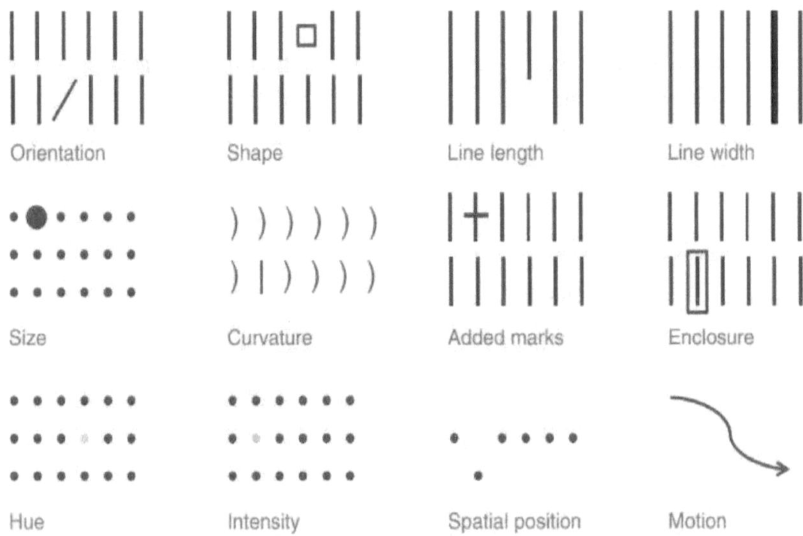

Nussbaumer Knaflic's Examples of Preattentive Attributes

Colour

Colour is one of the most important things to understand in data visualisation. Colour can be used to draw the attention of the reader, highlight a portion of data, or distinguish between different categories.

Some sample examples of the use of colour in data visualisations are as follows:

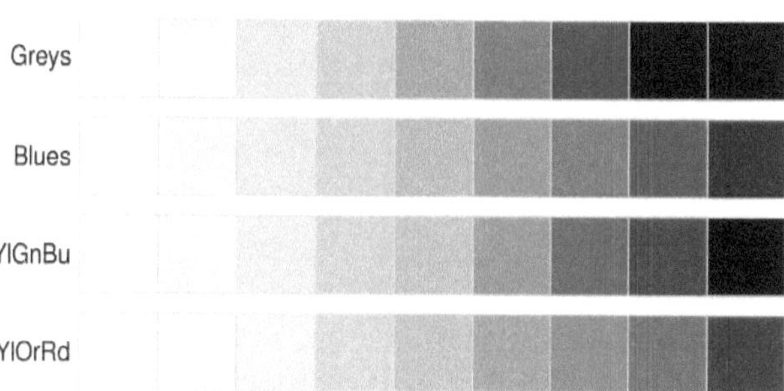

Sequential

Colour ordered from low to high

Sequential palettes

Greys

Blues

YlGnBu

YlOrRd

Diverging

Two sequential colour with neutral midpoint

Diverging palettes

RdYlBu

RdBu

PuOr

BrBG

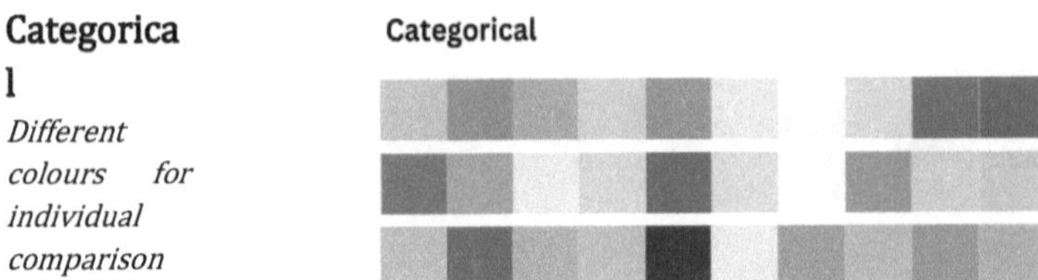

Categorica l
Different colours for individual comparison

Highlight
Colours use to highlight somethings

Special Positioning

Spatial Relations is the ability to perceive two or more object's position in space relative to oneself and in relation to each other. The main pre-attentive attributes for spatial positioning are:

- 2D Positioning
- Stereoscopic depth
- Concave/convex positioning

Motion: Motion is easy and one of the best ways to get our brain's attention but at the same time it creates a distraction. Traffic light is a common example for motion pre-attentive attributes.

Common Chart Types

In this section, we will cover different types of charts. We will explain why a particular chart is useful for a particular task.

Various tools and techniques are available that are used to convert the data in its visual form which cannot be directly converted by human beings e.g. Microsoft excel, or spreadsheets are commonly used for small sets of data. Some of the traditional data visualisation techniques to represent data are bar charts, line charts, pie charts, scatter charts, bubble charts, area charts, heatmap etc.

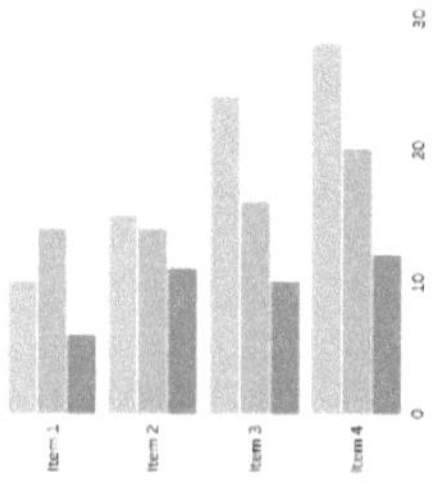

Bar Charts are most commonly used for comparing quantities of different categories or groups. The bar could be vertical or horizontal and represent the value of a category.

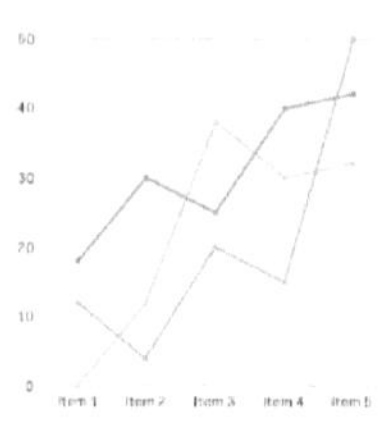

Line Charts show the relationship of one variable to another. Most commonly used to track changes or trends over time. Line charts are also useful for comparing multiple items over the same time period

Waterfall Chart: Another bar chart called as progressive bar chart or waterfall chart. A waterfall chart shows how the initial value of a measure increases or decreases during a time timeframe. The first bar is the initial value and the rest bar indicates the magnitude of type (positive, negative) of the operation.

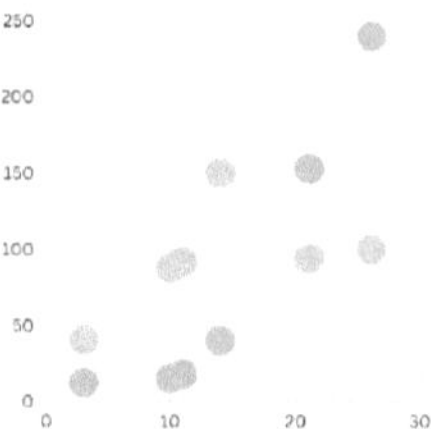

Scattered Chart uses dots to represent values for two numerical variables. The position of each dot on the horizontal and vertical axis indicates values for individual data points. Scatter plots can help you gain a sense of how data is spread and closely related to each other. Scatter plot useful for examining the relationship or relationship between X and Y variables. Variables are said to be correlated if they have a dependency on or show any influence by each other. Scattered plot generally uses in statistical analysis like regression, identify

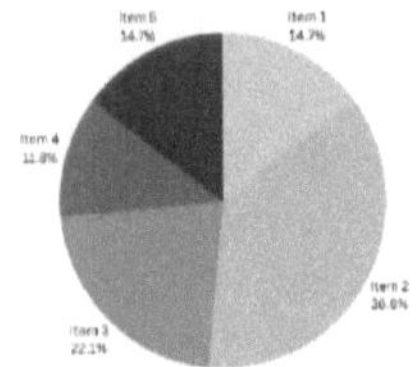

Pie Chart: Emphasising differences in proportion among a few numbers, pie chart or donut chart are most commonly used when there are limited components and when text and percentage are included to describe the content.

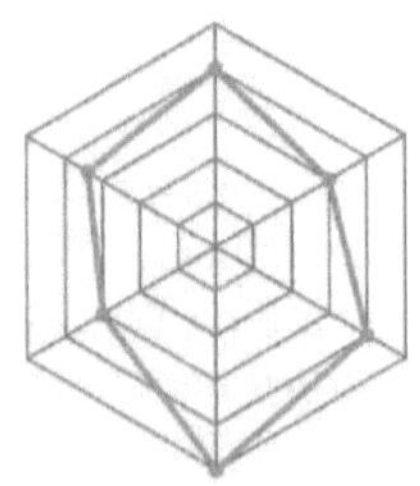

Radar Chart, sometimes called spider chart, is a way of comparing multiple quantitative variables across several unique dimensions. Each dimension's range is normalised to one another, so that when we draw our spider chart, the length of a line from zero to a dimension's maximum value will be the same for every dimension. All axes are arranged radially, with equal distances between each other, while maintaining the same scale between all axes.

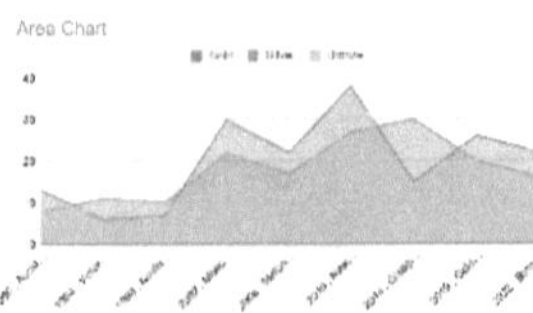

The area graph is the same as the line graph, just the area below the line is filled with specific colours. The best case scenario is that your data series never crosses over one another, so that the chart looks like a mountain range where all peaks are visible. More likely, at least once in your chart you'll see data series cross over one another, and then you will inevitably have hidden data.

Stack Area Chart:

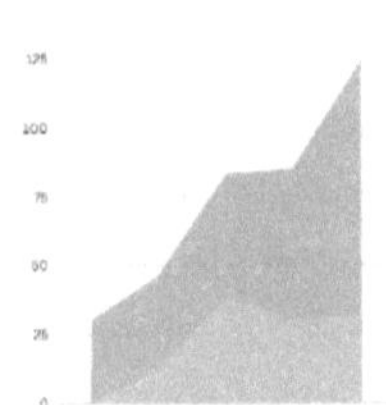

Stacked Area Chart is similar to the simple area chart, but here it uses multiple data series that start each point from the point left by the previous series. It is useful for comparing multiple variables changing over an interval. The entire graph represents the total of all the data plotted. Stacked Area Graphs also use the areas to convey whole numbers, so they do not work for negative values. Overall, they are useful for comparing multiple variables changing over an interval.

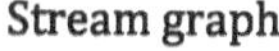
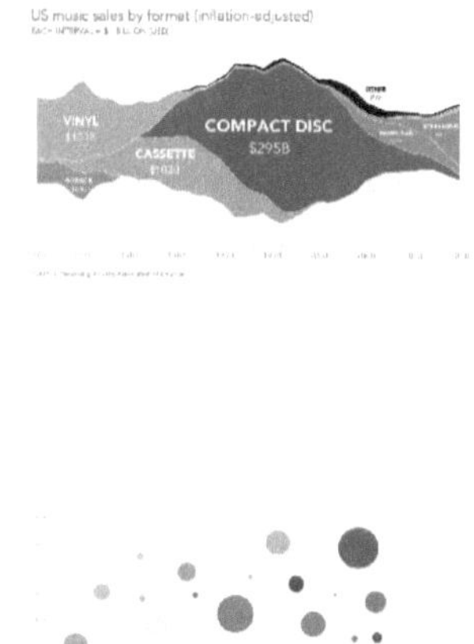

Stream graph

Stream graph is a variation of a Stacked Area Graph, but instead of plotting values against a fixed, straight axis, a Stream Graph has values displaced around a varying central baseline. Stream graphs display the changes in data over time of different categories through the use of flowing, organic shapes that somewhat resemble a river-like stream.

The Bubble chart is commonly used to visualise relationships between three or more numeric variables. Each bubble in a chart represents a single data point. The values for each bubble are encoded by 1) its horizontal position on the x-axis, 2) its vertical position on the y-axis, and 3) the size of the bubble. Colours can also be used to distinguish between categories or used to represent an additional data variable. Bubble charts are typically used to compare and show the relationships between categorised circles, by the use of positioning and proportions. The overall picture of bubble charts can be used to analyse patterns/correlations.

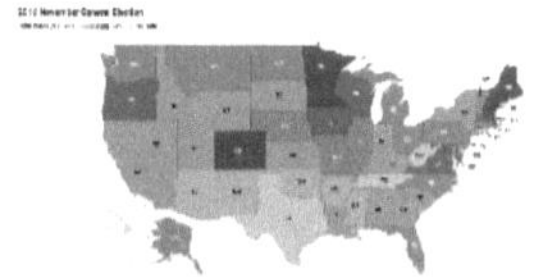

Choropleth Maps

Display divided geographical areas or regions that are coloured, shaded or patterned in relation to a data variable. This provides a way to visualise values over a geographical area, which can show variations or patterns across the displayed location. The data variable uses colour progression to represent itself in each region of the map. Typically, this can be a blending from one colour to another, a single hue progression, transparent to opaque, light to dark or an entire colour spectrum.

Dot map

Dot maps are a way of detecting spatial patterns or the distribution of data over a geographical region, by placing equally sized points over a geographical region. A dot plot can reveal patterns when the points cluster on the map. Two types of Dot maps: 1) one-to-one (one point represents a single object) and 2) one-to-many (one point represents multiple objects).

Connection Maps are drawn by connecting points placed on a map by straight or curved lines.

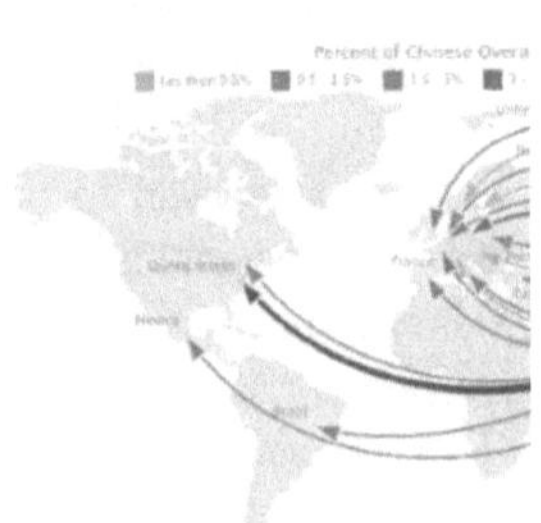

Flow Map

Flow maps geographically show the movement of information or objects from one location to another and their amount. Typically, flow maps are used to show the migration data of people, animals and products.

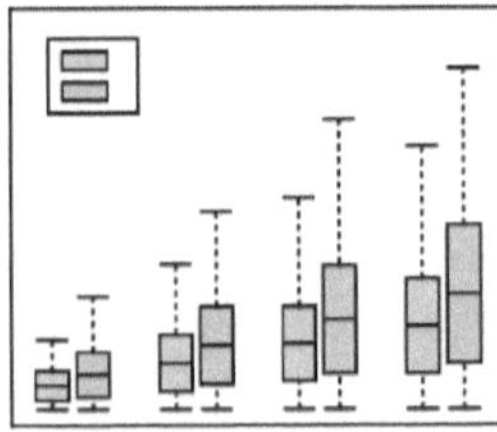

Box and Whisker Plot is also called a box plot also named as a five-number summary of a set of data. Box and whisker plots are very effective and easy to read, as they can summarise data from multiple sources and display the results in a single graph. Box and whisker plots allow for the comparison of data from different categories for easier, more effective decision-making.

The five-number summary divides the data into sections that each contain approximately 25% of the data in that set.

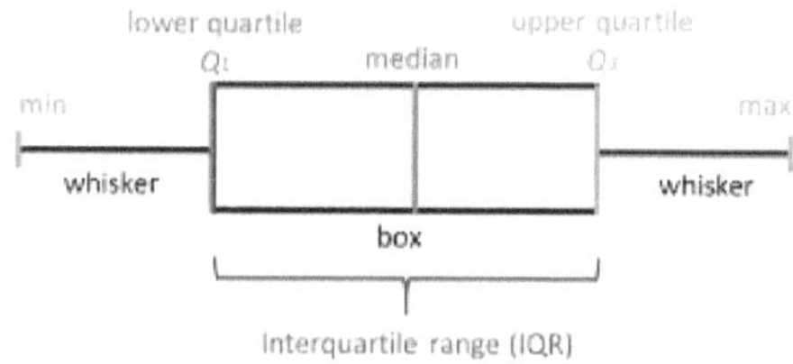

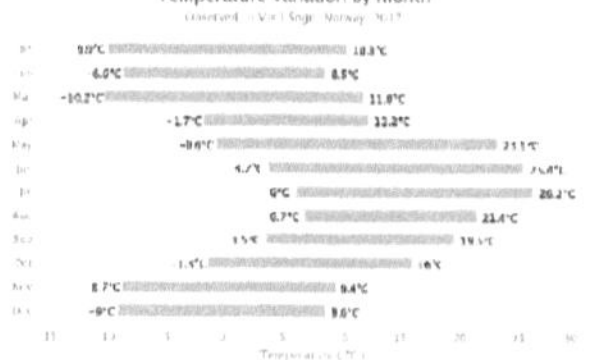

Span Char

Also known as range bar/ column bar. A chart used to display dataset ranges between a minimum value and a maximum value. Span charts are ideal for comparing ranges, typically for categorised ranges. It looks like a box, the upper edge of the box indicates a maximum, whereas the lower edge of the box indicates a minimum.

CandleStick Chart

Candlestick charts are used by traders to determine possible price movement based on past patterns. CandleStick chart more resemble Box plots but they function differently. Candlestick charts display multiple bits of price information such as open price, close price, highest price and lowest price.

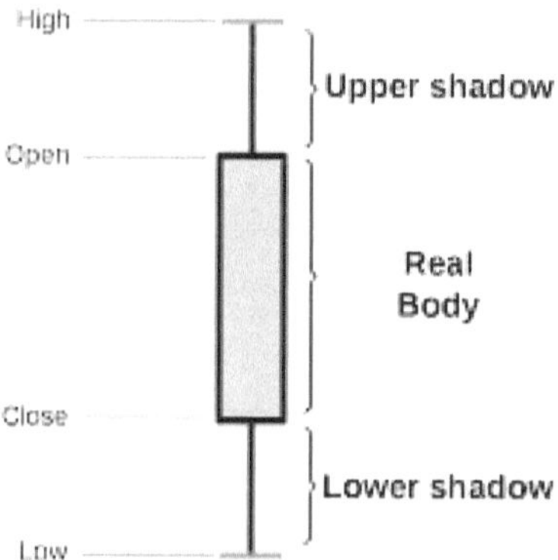

Gantt Chart

Commonly used as an organisational tool for project management, Gantt Charts display a list of activities (or tasks) with their duration over time, showing when each activity starts and ends. This makes Gantt charts useful for planning and estimating how long an entire project might take. You can also see what activities are running in parallel to each other. Gantt charts are drawn within a table: rows are used for the activities and columns are used as the timescale. The duration of each activity is represented by the length of a bar plotted along this timescale.

The start of the bar is the beginning of the activity and the end of the bar is when the activity should finish. Colour-coding the bars can be used to categorise the activities into groups. To show the percentage of completion of an activity, a bar can be partially filled in, shaded differently or used in a different colour, to differentiate between what is done and what is left to do.

Network Diagram

Network diagrams (also called Graphs) show interconnections between a set of entities. Each entity is represented by a Node (or vertice). Connections between nodes are represented through links (or edges). This type of visualisation shows how things are interconnected. The two notable types of network diagrams are "undirected" and "directed". Undirected Network Diagrams only display the connections between entities, while directed network diagrams show if the connections are one-way or two-way through small arrows.

Arc Diagram

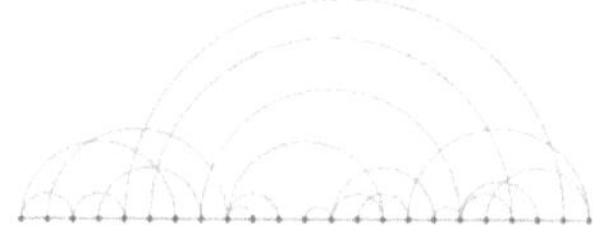

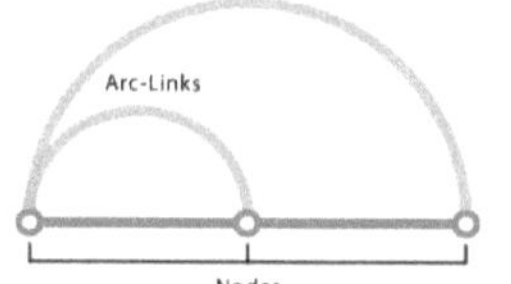

Arc diagram is a special kind of network diagram. In Arc Diagrams, nodes are placed along a single line (a one-dimensional axis) and arcs are used to show connections between those nodes. The thickness of each arc line can be used to represent the frequency between the source and target node. Arc diagrams can be useful in finding the co-occurrence within the data.

Histogram

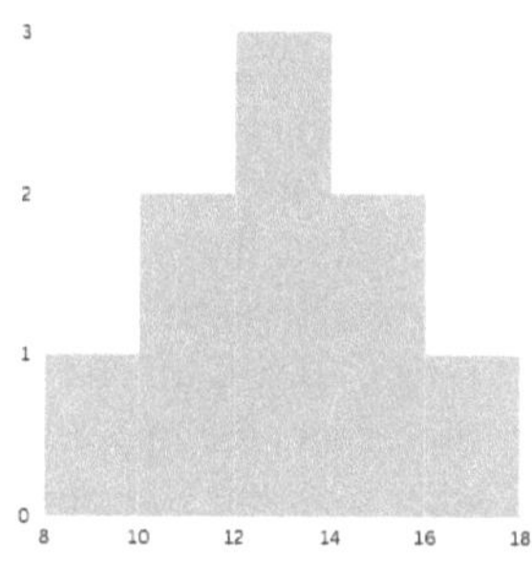

A histogram is a graphical display of data using bars of different heights. In a histogram, each bar groups numbers into ranges. Taller bars show that more data falls in that range. A histogram visualises the distribution of data over a continuous interval or certain time period. Histograms help give an estimate as to where values are concentrated, what the extremes are and whether there are any gaps or unusual values. They are also useful for giving a rough view of the probability distribution.

Density Plot

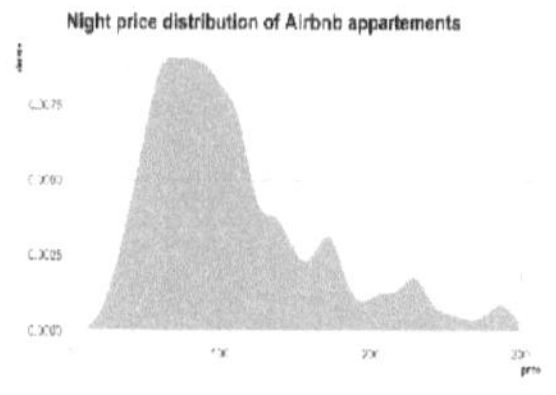

It is a smoothed version of the histogram. A density plot is a representation of the distribution of a numeric variable that uses a kernel density estimate to show the probability density function of the variable.

An advantage density plots have over Histograms is that they're better at determining the distribution shape.

Population Pyramid

Also known as Age and Sex pyramid

This is a two-layer bar graph, which can be used to present the population pyramid about males and females in a certain year. So, by

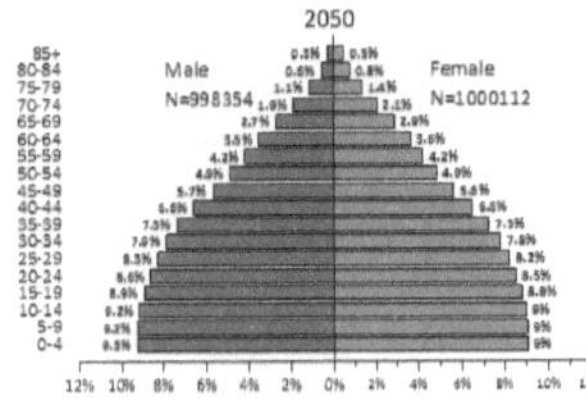

default, the two data columns should contain the population numbers of the male and females respectively. The X-axis is used to plot population numbers and the Y-axis lists all age groups. Population Pyramids are ideal for detecting changes or differences in population patterns. Multiple Population Pyramids can be used to compare patterns across nations or selected population groups.

Violin Plot

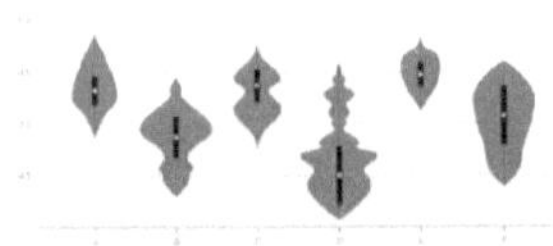

A Violin Plot is used to visualise the distribution of the data and its probability density.

This chart is a combination of a Box Plot and a Density Plot that is rotated and placed on each side, to show the distribution shape of the data. The white dot in the middle is the median value and the thick black bar in the centre represents the interquartile range. The thin black line extending from it represents the upper (max) and lower (min) adjacent values in the data. Sometimes the graph marker is clipped from the end of this line.

Radial / Circular Bar Chart

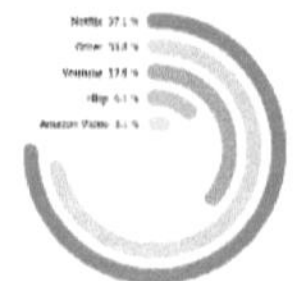

A Radial/Circular Bar Chart is simply a Bar Chart plotted on a polar coordinate system, rather than on a Cartesian one.

Radial Column Chart

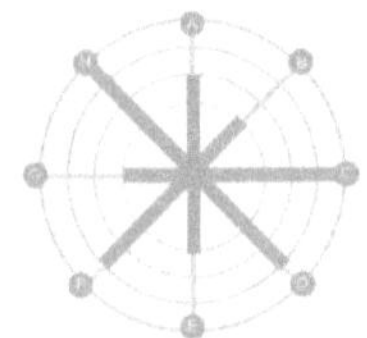

Also called the Star graph.

The bars on this chart are plotted on a grid of concentric circles, each representing a value on a scale. Usually, the inner circles represent lower values and values increase as you move outward. Sometimes each bar is further divided using colour to show subgroups within each category.

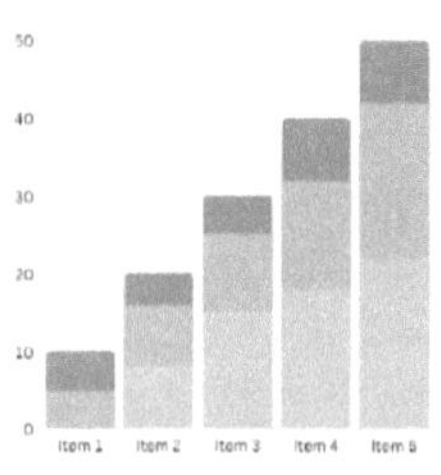

Stacked Bar Chart

The stacked bar chart extends the standard bar chart from looking at numeric values across one categorical variable to two. Stacked Bar Graphs are used to show how a larger category is divided into smaller categories and what the relationship of each part has on the total amount.

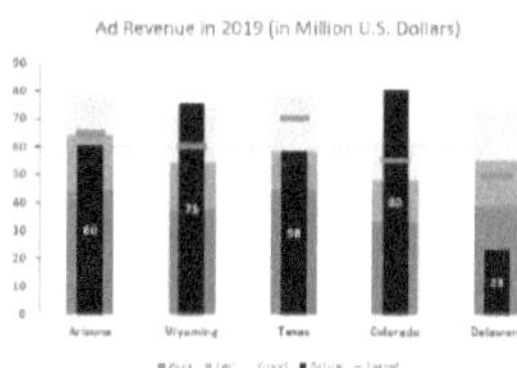

Bullet Graph

A bullet graph is a variation of a bar graph developed to replace dashboard gauges and metres. A bullet graph is useful for comparing the performance of a primary measure to one or more other measures. The main data value is encoded by the length of the main bar in the middle of the chart, known as the Feature Measure. The line marker that runs perpendicular to the orientation of the graph is known as the Comparative Measure and is used as a target marker to compare against the Feature Measure value. The segmented coloured bars behind the Feature Measure are used to display qualitative range scores. Each colour shade (the three shades of grey in the example above) is used to assign a performance range rating.

Marimekko chart

A Marimekko chart is a graphical representation that uses stacked bar graphs of varying widths to visualise categorical data. A Marimekko chart is also known as a mosaic plot, or simply, Mekko chart. They are ideal for representing categorical sample data. In a Marimekko Chart, both axes are variable with a percentage scale that determines both the width and height of each segment.

Tree Map

Treemap charts depict data in a tree-like format, with branches and sub-branches that are able to be read at a glance. Each category is assigned a rectangle area with its subcategory rectangles nested inside of it.

Sunburst diagram

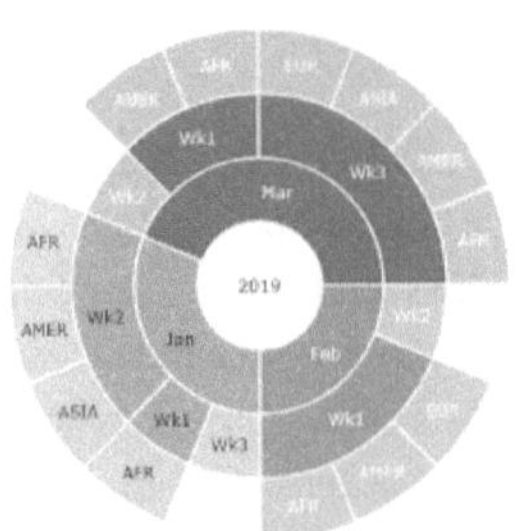

A sunburst diagram displays a hierarchical structure. The origin of the organisation is represented by the centre of the circle, and each level of the organisation by an additional ring. The last level (leaves) is located at the extreme outer part of the circle.

Chord Diagram

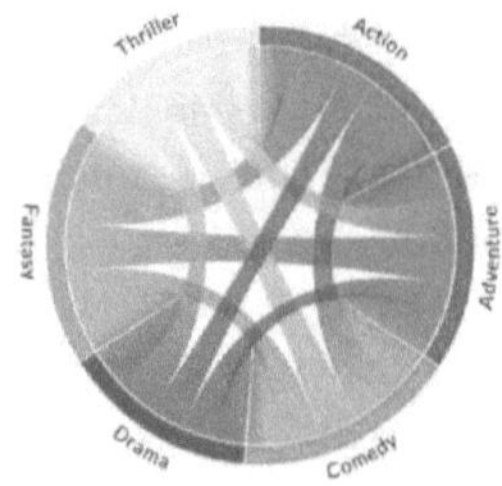

A chord diagram represents flows or connections between several entities (called nodes). Each entity is represented by a fragment on the outer part of the circular layout. Then, arcs are drawn between each entity. The size of the arc is proportional to the importance of the flow.

Non-ridden Chord diagram

Compared to traditional Chord diagrams, Non-ribbon chord diagrams emphasise the connections between data points rather than additional properties of those connections.

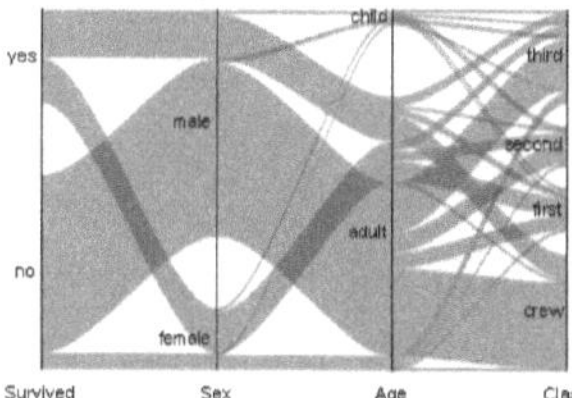

Parallel Set

Parallel plot or Parallel Coordinates plot allows the comparison of the features of several individual observations on a set of numeric variables. Each vertical bar represents a variable and usually has its own scale.

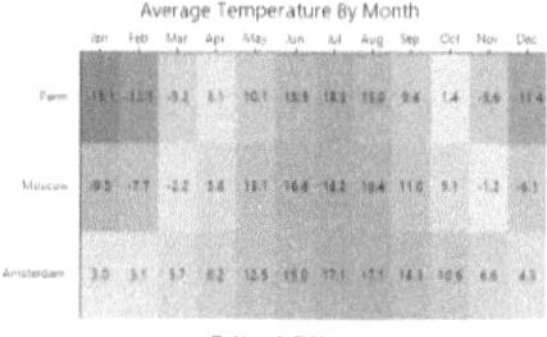

Heatmap

A heatmap is a graphical representation of data where the individual values contained in a matrix are represented as colours. Heatmaps are good for showing variance across multiple variables, revealing any patterns, displaying whether any variables are similar to each other, and for detecting if any correlations exist in-between them.

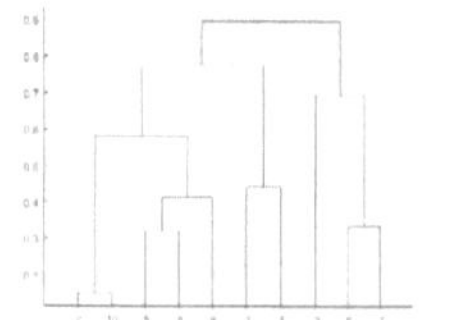

Dendrogram

A dendrogram is a network structure. It is constituted of a root node that gives birth to several nodes connected by edges or branches.

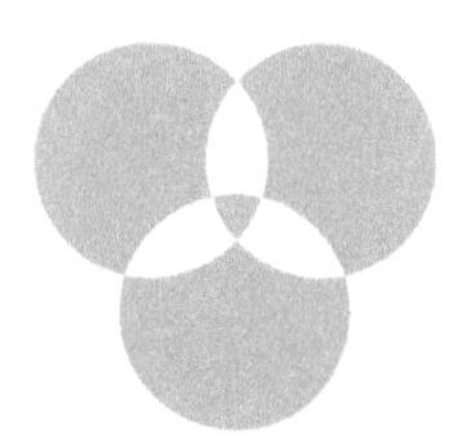

Venn Diagram

A Venn diagram is a diagram that shows all possible logical relationships between a collection of sets. Each set is represented by a circle. The circle size represents the importance of the group. The groups are usually overlapping: the size of the overlap represents the intersection between both groups.

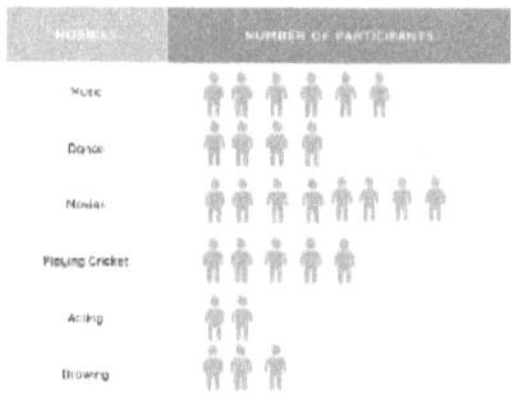

Pictogram Chart

Pictogram Charts use icons to give a more engaging overall view of small sets of discrete data. Typically, the icons represent the data's subject or category, for example, data on population would use icons of people. Each icon can represent one unit or any number of units.

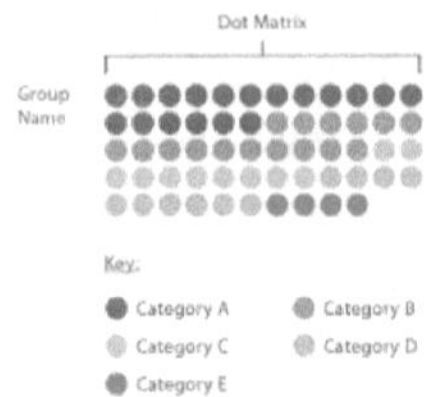

Dot Matrix

Dot Matrix Charts display discrete data in units of dots, each coloured to represent a particular category and grouped together in a matrix. They are used to give a quick overview of the distribution and proportions of each category in a data set and also to compare distribution and proportion across other datasets, in order to discover patterns.

Word Count

A visualisation method that displays how frequently words appear in a given body of text, by making the size of each word proportional to its frequency. All the words are then arranged in a cluster or cloud of words.

TimeLine

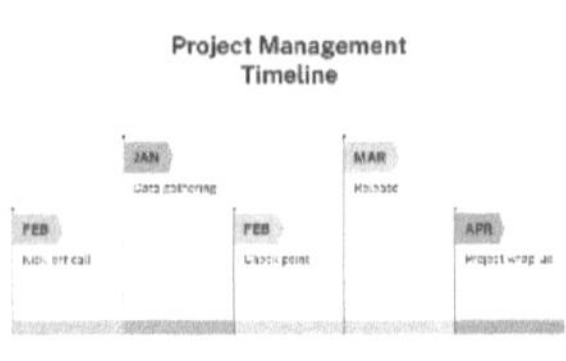

A Timeline is a graphical way of displaying a list of events in chronological order. Some timelines work on a scale, while others simply display events in a sequence.

Data Visualization for Business Executive

A data dashboard is an interactive analysis tool used by businesses to track and monitor the performance of their strategies with quality KPIs. People think of a dashboard in many different ways, but in short, it is a collection of data visualisations or metrics giving insight into a set of business questions. Dashboard should provide answers to Key Business KPIs and highlight current trends and patterns.

In today's business world dashboard is categorised in four types:
- Operational dashboard

- Analytical dashboard
- Strategic dashboard
- Informational dashboard

Operational dashboards: An operational dashboard is used to monitor the performance of different business operations. It monitors business trends and patterns. These dashboards are responsive, dynamic, and effective for in-the-moment decision-making.

Analytical dashboards: typically used by the senior executive and decision makers. This kind of dashboard provides more drill-down information about particular events or provides top-level perspective for business executives.

Strategic dashboards: are used for tracking long-term company strategy with the help of critical success factors. Generally, a strategic dashboard is designed on an enterprise level.

Informational dashboard: Informational dashboards are usually focused on a very specific process or branch of information and are effective for gaining useful at-a-glance data or short-term strategic decision-making.

Let's take an example of a management dashboard(analytic dashboard) and understand how it helps to provide answers to business KPIs.

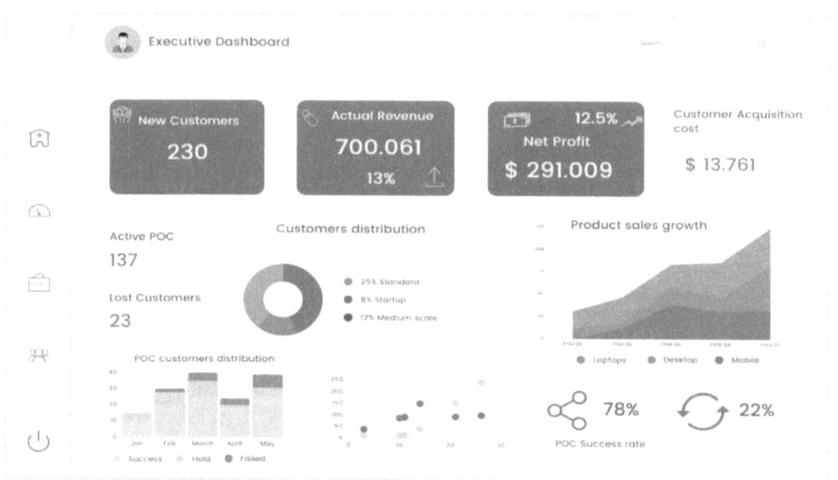

Big picture

Management dashboards are extremely useful when strategic decision-making processes need to summarise. It gives a real-time overview of what's happening in the business. As a business executive, you need to overview the current and historical trends of your business sales and growth.

Use cases
- What's customer distribution?
- What's the current profit range?
- What's the sales distribution?
- What's the customer churn rate?

How people use this dashboard
This dashboard is designed to provide a complete view of business insight across different regions, product ,and customer distributions.

Different components of dashboard

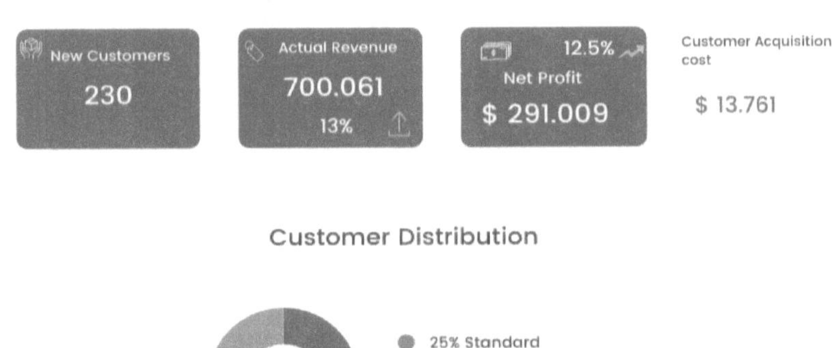

Our management dashboard example focuses on revenue in total, plus the cost of acquiring new customers. It delivers this information by providing you with information regarding total revenue and net profit growth, as well as statistics relating to the number of new customers and customer acquisition cost.

If you are looking for a broad overview of your customer types and distribution. This graph tells you about customer segmentation.

- Chart Type - **Donut chart**
- Data - categorical data
- Different customer segmentations identify with different unique colours.

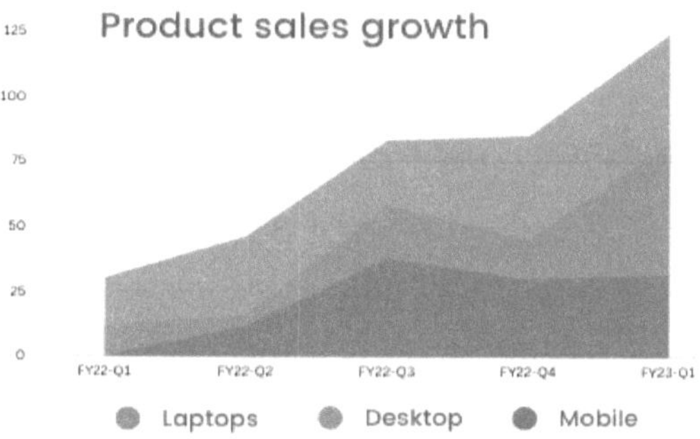

One of the most important KPI for any product based companies is how their product sales perform over the years.

- Chart - Stack Area
- Data - categorical data
- Preattentive Attributes - Color

POC status

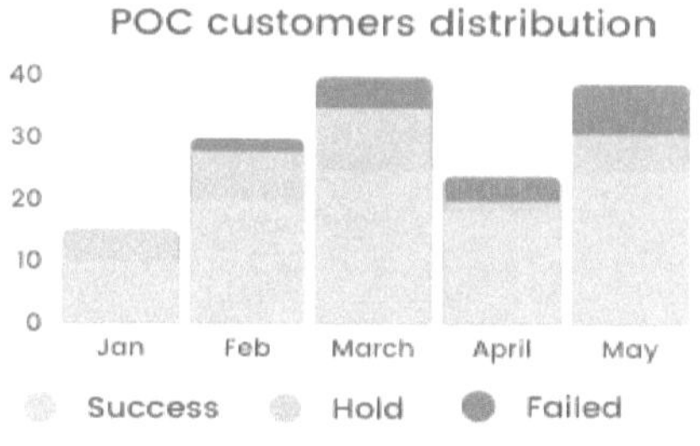

This section focuses on POC customers' status, you want to keep a high percentage on the successful POC win, and failed rate as low as possible.

- Chart - Stacked Bar Graph
- Data - Categorical

- o   Success
- o   Hold
- o   Failed

Data Storytelling

Data Storytelling is not a new concept, it is an old method but widely used in industry nowadays. It's the ability to effectively communicate insight from a dataset using narratives and visualisations.

There are three components of data storytelling:

- **Data**: It is the foundation for your story. Different analysis approaches like descriptive, diagnostic, predictive and prescriptive can enable you to understand the full picture.

- **Narrative**: It's a kind of storyline, the way you would like to communicate your message to the audience. Narrative helps to build context surrounding the data and provides clear insight from your data.

- **Visualisation**: This helps to visualise your message very clearly and memorably. These can be charts, graphs, diagrams, pictures or videos etc.

Here are some examples of how mapping police violence utilised the power of data storytelling to communicate their facts:

Research in Police Violence

Data visualisation is not only restricted to business analysis purposes but it is also used in many other ways. In an article, mapping police violence source (www. mappingpoliceviolence.org) research information published on police violence show that "blacks" are approximately three times more likely to be killed in comparison to their "white" counterparts (mapping police violence, 2022). Additionally, it is worth noting that 97%

of the killings in our database occurred while a police officer was acting in a law enforcement capacity.

Police violence research visualises is a good example of preattentive variables utilisation.

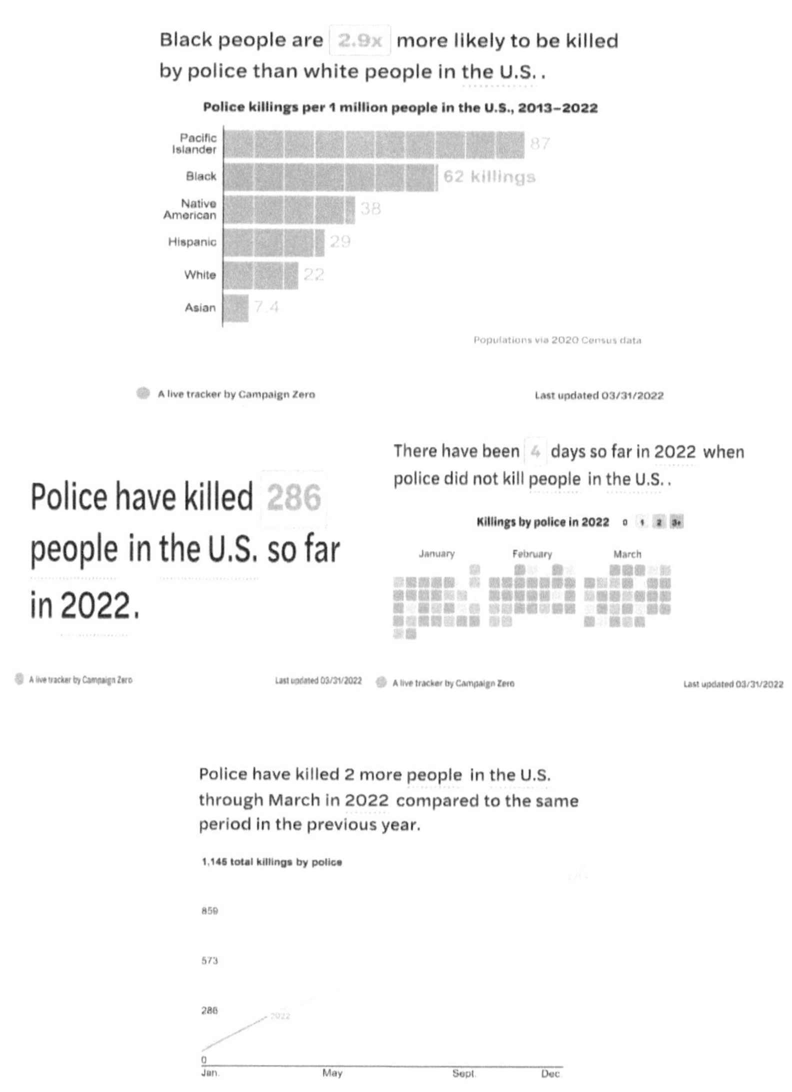

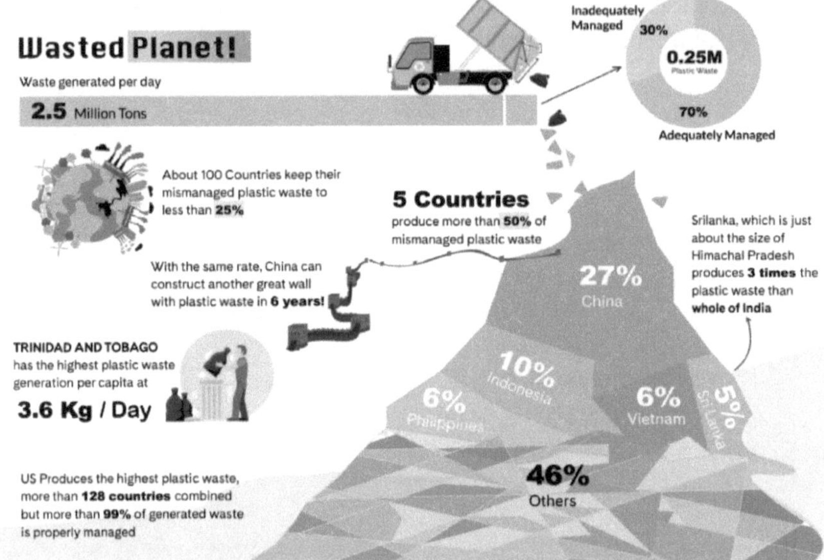

Let's have another example for data storytelling
What message is communicating with the image here ?

Major highlights are narrated that includes-

> 5 countries in the world are responsible for generating 50% of the data.

> China and Indonesia are major contributors for the waste generation.

We generate 2.5 million tons of waste every day.

Plastic waste is a major concern area for the US and other countries and more than 100 countries are not in position to manage plastic waste.

Whatever the story the data tells, it has to be communicated very effectively with a good narrative, the audience should connect easily and understand the message very effectively.

Data Visualization Tools

I am highlighting some most popular data visualisation tools, obviously the list is much bigger than listed below.

- **D3.js**: This is a JavaScript library for producing dynamic, interactive data visualisations in web browsers.

- **Candela**: As an open-source suite of web visualisation components that make use of the Python language, Candela emphasises scalable, rich visualisations created with a normalised API for use in real-world data science situations

- **Chartbuilder:** With Chartbuilder's intuitive web-based application, creating charts and diagrams is a matter of copy and paste. Easy-to-understand buttons and settings, as well as a consistent display showing what your visualisations look like on mobile and desktop browsers, allow for a clean user experience.

- **Charted:** It is an open-source tool that automatically visualises data. All you have to do is provide a link to a data file and the tool will return a shareable visualisation of that data.

- **Chartist.js:** This includes a large array of charts that are responsive, animated, and rendered beautifully.

- **Datawrapper** is an extremely easy-to-use data visualisation tool for plotting interactive charts. All you need to do is upload your data via a CSV file, choose the chart you want to plot. It's free and no sign-up is needed.

- **Dygraphs:** It is a JavaScript charting library that allows for panning, zooming, and mouse-over actions. It handles and interprets dense datasets very effectively.

- **Leaflet** is an open-source JavaScript library for mobile-friendly interactive maps. One of the best parts about this tool is that it is extremely lightweight.

- **RAW Graphs:** The idea behind RAW Graphs is to provide a way to easily explore your data and create visualisation without coding skills. The framework is built on the D3.js library and is built in such a way that even non-programmers can use it with ease.

- **Polymaps**: As its name suggests, Polymaps is for creating cartographic data visualisations. It pulls in data from OpenStreetMap, Bing, and other map image providers, while also rendering its own representations.

- **Power BI** is a business intelligence and data visualisation tool which helps you to convert data from various data sources into interactive dashboards and reports. It provides multiple software connectors and services.

- **Tableau** is a robust tool for visualising data in a better way. You can connect any database to create understandable visuals. It is one of the best visualisation tools that enables you to share visualisation with other people.

- **TimelineJS** is a great tool for creating interactive, visually rich timelines without having to write code. TimelineJS has built-in API support for a variety of data sources like Wikipedia, Twitter, SoundCloud, Vine, Google Maps, and YouTube.

- **Microsoft PowerBI**: The Microsoft Power BI is the data visualisation tool that is used for business intelligence type of data. It is and can be used for reporting, self-service analytics and predictive analytics.

- **Quikview**: Has good options available to visualise information. It is loaded with various objects. You can play with properties of these objects easily to customise it.

- **Matplotlib**: Matplotlib is a cross-platform, data visualisation and graphical plotting library for Python and its numerical extension NumPy. As such, it offers a viable open source alternative to MATLAB. Developers can also use matplotlib's APIs (Application Programming Interfaces) to embed plots in GUI applications.

Summary

In this chapter, we tried to cover an overview of data visualisation and its key benefits. Visualisation helps to expedite the decision making process. It helps to understand data better and in an easy way. We also covered preattentive attributes. Pre-attentive attributes are eye catcher and it is very useful highlighting certain key information with the help of these techniques.

This chapter also helped you to understand different types of charts and graphs. Depending on the scenarios different graphs and charts are used.

Talkies about data storytelling with examples, it has three important comentens that includes data, narrative and visualisation.

We discussed different components of the dashboard and explained to you how charts are indeed to represent valuable information.

References

- https://ufs.libguides.com/c.php?g=977378&p=7263744
- https://www.lucidchart.com/blog/the-power-of-real-time-data-visualization
- https://datascience.aero/brain-data-visualization/
- https://ufs.libguides.com/c.php?g=977378&p=7263744
- https://www.datapine.com/blog/data-dashboards-definition-examples-templates/

Nine

Safeguard your Data

DATA PROTECTION

Think of data protection as an insurance policy. In that sense, the aim of data protection is not to maximise profits or revenues, or to minimise costs, but to minimise worst-case losses. Like other insurance, data protection insurance is a necessary cost of the prudent business, and it balances the costs of unplanned outages against the costs of the insurance policy.

— *Book*" Data Protection - by David G. Hill

Introduction

How many times have you heard about data breaches, cyber or ransomware attacks? I guess almost everyday. More and more companies and individuals experience crippling data breaches.

Security is a major concern for most of the companies that collect or share data. When data is collected for customer profiling, user behaviour understanding, correlating personal data with other information, etc. large amounts of sensitive and private information about individuals or companies is gathered and stored. Companies collect large amounts of data and process it at every stage. With such an enormous amount of data, it has become important that government bodies (local, national or global) take necessary steps to protect the data rights of their citizens. According to the Data Protection Acts 2018 under General Data Protection Regulation (GDPR), everyone responsible for using personal data has to follow strict rules called data protection principles. They must make sure that the information is

- used fairly, lawfully and transparently
- used for specified, explicit purposes

- used in a way that is adequate, relevant and limited to only what is necessary
- accurate and, where necessary, kept up to date
- kept for no longer than is necessary
- handled in a way that ensures appropriate security, including protection against unlawful or unauthorised processing, access, loss, destruction or damage.

Before we jump onto data protection, let's understand types of data. Data are generally divided into two categories:

- Sensitive Data
- Public Data

- **Public Data**: Public data is information that can be freely used, reused and redistributed by anyone with no existing local, national or international legal restrictions on access or usage. Public data includes-
  - Your social media post
  - Government data freely available on sites
  - Any Press releases
  - Job descriptions
  - Company details

- **Sensitive Data**: The exposure of sensitive data is potentially harmful and can lead to major losses for individuals or organisations if the right measures aren't taken to prevent unwarranted disclosure. Sensitive data can be classified into-
  - Personal information
  - Business Information
  - Classified information

- **Personal information**: It is any piece of information that relates to or can be related to a natural person that can be directly or indirectly identified via that information. This includes your
  - First Name, Last Name
  - email address
  - phone number
  - home address

- IP address etc
  You can't always find individuals by first name, last name but combining those details with location or phone number could identify individuals.

- **Business Information**: If business information is released to the public, competitors can use this type of sensitive information to their advantage. It's important to understand the type of information you collect, why you collect it, and how you can ensure this sensitive data remains protected.
    - Financial data
    - Trade secrets
    - Supplier information
    - Customer data

- **Classified Information**: Classified information is restricted, confidential, secret, or top secret information kept private at a high or government level based on country laws and restrictions. Access to this type of information is only given to certain individuals with the proper authorization and security clearance.

What is Data Protection ?

Data protection is the process of protecting sensitive information from damage, loss or corruption and ensuring that customers trust you to use their data fairly and responsibly.

If any company collects any personal information about individuals then the company needs to comply.

Data protection is extremely important for business continuity, even short periods of downtime or small amounts of data loss can have major consequences on a business. Data protection helps reduce risk and enables a business to respond quickly to threats.

Data steal with numerous way few of them includes:

Malware: Malware is any type of malicious software. It may be designed to harvest and exfiltrate data, make an operating system unusable or otherwise disrupt the target device. Subtypes of malware include spyware, trojans, worms, viruses, and ransomware. According to McAfee, cybercriminals use malware for-

- Tricking a victim into providing personal data for identity theft.

- Stealing consumer credit card data or other financial data.

- Assuming control of multiple computers to launch denial-of-service attacks against other networks.

- Infecting computers and using them to mine bitcoin or other cryptocurrencies.

- **Ransomware**: One of the most profitable, and therefore one of the most popular, types of malware amongst cybercriminals is ransomware. Ransomware is a type of malware that prevents or limits users from accessing their system, either by locking the system's screen or by locking the users' files until a ransom is paid.

- **Phishing**: Phishing is a type of social engineering attack often used to steal user data, including login credentials and credit card numbers. Phishing messages manipulate a user, causing them to perform actions like installing a malicious file, clicking a malicious link, or divulging sensitive information such as access credentials.
E.g. The email claims that the user's password is about to expire. Instructions are given as- login to university - xdfgff.com/renewal.com within 24 hours.

Why is Data Protection important?

India recently banned 118 Chinese apps under the section 64A of the information technology act and it is due to illegal data practices followed by these apps. These apps were collecting extensive information about their users without taking explicit permission. Around the world, millions of dollars are fined due to non-compliance with regional data protection law.

Many organisations are handling more and more data. Bad actors, outside an organisation and inside of it, constantly look to compromise an organisation's data security for their own ends. Data breaches often aim to steal information from a company,

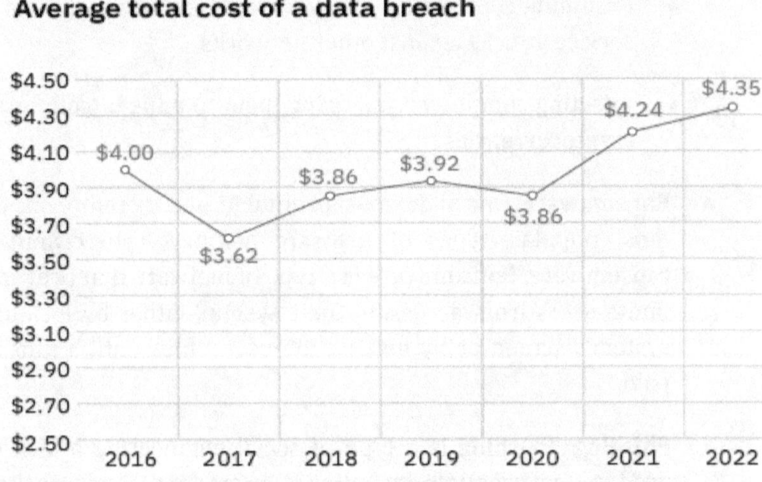

According to IBM's Global Cost to Breach report -2022, global average total cost of a data breach is around USD 4.35 million dollar, increased by 2.6% compared to year 2021.In the last two years, the average total cost has increased 12.7% from USD 3.86 million in the 2020 report.

Since organisations handle a great deal of personal identifiable information (PII) from their customers, employees, and stakeholders, a data breach can do a great deal of harm.

Data Protection spectrum

Data protection touches a wide spectrum of business issues, including but by no means limited to:

- Data Availability (Business continuity)
- Data Security
- Data Compliance
- Governance

Data Protection

Protection Categories	Techniques
Data Protection for Business continuity	<ul><li>Backup - Restore</li><li>RAID techniques</li><li>Data Archiving</li><li>Data Replication</li><li>Data Retention</li><li>Data Immutability</li><li>Infrastructure - High Availability</li></ul>
Data Security	<ul><li>Access Control</li><li>Encryption</li><li>Obfuscation or Masking</li><li>Multi Factor Authentication</li><li>Data Activity Monitoring</li><li>Data Loss Prevention</li><li>Sensitivity Labels</li><li>Network Security</li><li>Device security</li><li>Facility Security</li></ul>

Data Privacy

- Geographical Regulation
- Data Classification
- Data De-identification
- Anonymisation

Data Availability

Data availability is important for business continuity. Effective business continuity protects key stakeholders' interests, brand reputation, the goodwill of customers, and the value-creating activities of the enterprise. If a business continuity strategy fails, the consequences can range from undesirable or unacceptable (customer dissatisfaction or loss of productivity) to severe (economic loss of market valuation/revenue or loss of public or customer confidence), to outright catastrophic (business failure).

It is important to understand what can cause your data to become inaccessible and what challenges you overcome to protect your data.

Business continuity needs to mitigate following risks:
- Operational Risk
- Environmental Risk
- Application Risk
- Human Risk
- Cyber Risk

Operational Risk: When we talk about operational risk, it is mainly the ability to deal with day to day operational problems. Day to day operational business continuity requires the physical (storage device level) and logical (data itself) data protection. Both physical and logical data protection is important. If you have data available on a hard disk (physical devices) but it is corrupted then it won't be useful.

Operational Risk may cause due to multiple factors, that may includes following:

- Infra scaling issues
- Disk Failure
- Network congestion
- Application Performance
- Computer virus
- Hacking

Operation risk mitigation is within the control of the IT organisation.

Data loss can be avoided in operational risk using frequent point in time or incremental data backup that would copy and archive all essential business data and make it available in case of disaster or deletion.

Environmental Risk: Business continuity under environmental risk is to ensure essential business technology remains accessible and functional after, and optimally during, the occurrence of environmental disaster. Disaster could be cause by any reasons:

- Earthquake
- Blizzard
- Fire
- Flood

Disaster recovery facility is used to minimise the impact of a potential disaster. Operational continuity focuses on targeting individual problems, whereas disaster continuity has to focus on what would need to be done in the event that the entire IT infrastructure—including all applications and their supporting server, storage, and network services—has to be replicated at a site other than the original home of the applications. Disaster recovery not only involves recovering essential data but also in essential sets of hardware and software to continue processing of data and business.

Disaster recovery is possible when data processing has been moved from primary to a secondary site and when that processing is carried out using different types of computer hardware.

Many cloud based solutions and third party applications are available to protect a business's critical data against major disasters such as cyber-attack, natural disaster or accidental.

Application Risk: Application access is a prime gateway for others to access organisation or application data unethically. It is very important to keep your application secure and allow only authorised users. More than 58% of organisations are not aware that the data has been compromised through their application.

Texas Department of Insurance - Data Breach

On January 4, 2022, the Texas Department of Insurance (TDI) became aware of a security issue with a TDI web application that manages workers' compensation information. The audit report said confidential information related to workers' compensation claims may have been accessible to individuals outside the TDI between March 2019 and January 2022. The information at risk included claimants' names, addresses, dates of birth, and phone numbers; part or all of their Social Security numbers; and information about injuries and workers' compensation claims.

TDI said the data breach was caused by programming code that allowed internet access to a protected area of the application. After correcting the programming code, TDI placed the web application back online.

Many application tools are available in the market which helps to identify vulnerabilities and security issues.

Human Risk: To become a successful business continuity plan need ,right people with the right skills and knowledge. In his book "Modern Data Protection" W Curtis Preston mentioned that "The majority of restores and disaster recoveries today are executed because of humans doing something, accidentally or on purpose, that damages your computing environment."
The insider threat is a business risk created by anyone who has access to information about the firm's systems, processes, data, clients, or proprietary information assets.

Preventing human risk is critical from a business point of view from both external or internal threat. External can be avoided with applying right data protection policies against phishing, cybersecurity, application security. For insider threats, many companies don't have solid policies yet, and organisations should apply policies that restrict such events. Policies could be "minimum access data" where only authorised users should have data access. Data classification and only limit data access to specific users.

Cyber Risk : According to an annual cyber security report by Cisco, cyber criminals delivered a wave of cyber attacks that were not just highly coordinated, but far more advanced than ever before seen. Phishing, ransomware, social engineering, and trojans are the most active threads.

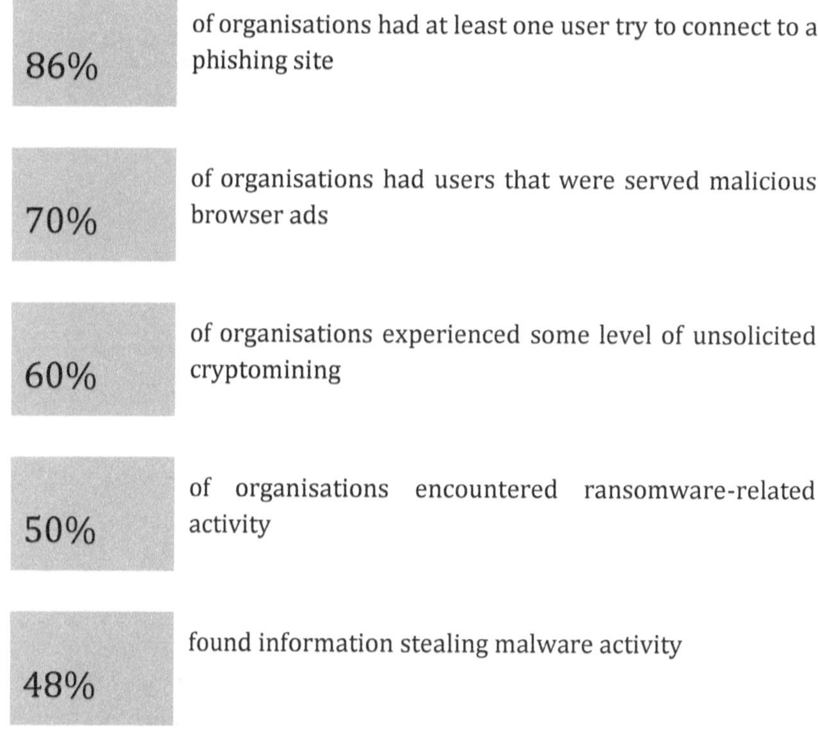

86% of organisations had at least one user try to connect to a phishing site

70% of organisations had users that were served malicious browser ads

60% of organisations experienced some level of unsolicited cryptomining

50% of organisations encountered ransomware-related activity

48% found information stealing malware activity

A successful cybersecurity approach has multiple layers of protection spread across the computers, networks, programs, or data that one intends to keep safe. In an organisation, the people, processes, and technology must all complement one another to create an effective defence from cyber attacks.

Data Protection techniques includes:

Backup and Restore

Backup & Restore works on logical data protection. Backup and Restore is the process of data duplication and storing it separately at a secure place from original copy.

Backup copy should be immutable and should not be altered after it is created to protect against any cyber attack. Backup can be taken onsite (on physical devices) or cloud storage.

The 3-2-1 strategy is the most widely used for backup strategy.

- Maintain at least 3 copies of your data
- Keep 2 copies stored at separate location
- Store at least 1 copy at off-site location or on cloud

Types of Backup

Full Backup: A full backup is the process of creating one or more copies of all organisational data files in a single backup operation to protect them.

Incremental Backup: An incremental backup captures only new data since the last full incremental was performed. However, a full backup is required before a backup solution can perform its first incremental backup.

Differential Backup: Differential and incremental backups are different backup strategies with the same purpose: optimise backup time and space. Differential backups only back up the files that have changed since the previous full backup, while incremental backups do the same, they back up the files that have changed since the previous incremental or full backup.

Recovery: Recovery is the process whereby you restore that backup data to a correct (consistent) state in the event of a failure.
Recovery can be granular level or entire data.

RAID Technology

Redundant Array of Independent Disk (RAID) deals with physical data protection. It is the first line of physical defence. RAID dramatically improved the availability of disk drives in a physical sense.

RAID combines multiple small, inexpensive disk drives into an array of disk drives which yields performance more than that of a Single Large Expensive Drive (SLED).

There are two types of RAID
- Software RAID
- Hardware RAID

Software RAID: Software RAID uses host-based software to provide RAID functions. It is implemented at the operating-system level and does not use a dedicated hardware controller to manage the RAID array.

Hardware RAID: In hardware RAID implementations, a specialised hardware controller is implemented either on the host or on the array.

Data Archiving

Data Archiving supports logical data protection. It is the practice of identifying and storing non active data into a separate long term storage system. In case of data loss, data archiving is intended for long-term retention of information that is no longer active, but which must be kept for historic, legal or compliance purposes.

Data Replication

Data replication supports physical as well as logical data protection and focus on business continuity, delivering uninterrupted operation of mission-critical and customer-facing applications after a disaster. Data replication is the process of storing the same data in multiple locations to improve data availability and accessibility, and to improve system resilience and reliability.

One common use of data replication is for disaster recovery, to ensure that an accurate backup exists at all times in case of a catastrophe, hardware failure, or a system breach where data is compromised.

Data Retention

Data retention is storing of information for a specified period. Data retention is primarily relevant to businesses that store data to service their customers and comply with government or industry regulations.

Health care organisations must develop data retention policies that adhere to the Health Insurance and Portability and Accountability Act (HIPAA). And any business that processes or stores personal information about EU citizens must comply with the General Data Protection Regulation (GDPR), whether or not they are member states.

Data Immutability

Immutability is the idea that data or objects should not be modified after they are created. Most traditional databases store data in a mutable format, meaning the database overwrites the older data when new data is available.

Many organisations choose to preserve their historical data for data privacy regulations. Data Immutability will help them to complain if a customer or government requests past data.

High Availability Infrastructure

HA Infrastructure supports physical data protection, and is a combination of hardware, software, and applications that are designed to recover quickly in case of outages and maintain functionalities in a way that assures minimum downtime and more than 99% availability.

Data Security

Data security refers to protecting your data against unauthorised access or use that could result in exposure, deletion, or corruption of that data. An example of data security would be using encryption to prevent hackers from using your data if it's breached.

- Access Control
- Encryption
- Obfuscation / Masking
- Network Security
- Device Security
- Data Retention

Access Control

Access control permits or denies the use of a particular operation on a particular system resource. Access control process includes:

- Authentication
- Authorization

- Auditing

Authentication: Authentication is the process of verifying a user or device before allowing access to a system or resources. Authentication is three steps process that includes,

- Identification—Who are you?
- Authentication—Prove it
- Authorization—Do you have permission?

Identification required user id or username. Authentication comes with pairing login id (user id / username) and password, authentication to confirm who you are. Most common authentication process is unique login and password. With an increase in cyber threat most organisations use additional precaution with multi factor authentication.

Authorization: Authorization in system security is the process of giving the user permission to access a specific resource or function.

For example, if you are the owner of the house, you have access to the entire home , you can move anywhere in the house and use all the resources. But if you have guests at your house it would be restricted to a particular area.

Auditing: Audit is the process of tracking and reviewing login user activities that includes events, errors, access and authentication attempts.

Encryption

Encryption is a vital component of data privacy and security. Data is transfermitted online (data in transit) and stored in the database (data in rest), and could hold personal information, financial information or any other business critical details. It is important to keep that information safe. Data encryption is the process through which data is encoded so that it remains hidden from or inaccessible to unauthorised users. Data encryption establishes secure communication between client apps and servers.

To encrypt data, an encryption key uses an encryption algorithm to translate plain texts or readable data into unreadable data or ciphertext. Only the corresponding description key can decode the unreadable or scrambled ciphertext back to readable plaintext.

There are four main methods of encryption - Hash, Symmetric, Private Key and Public Key.

Hash Key: Hash encryption uses algorithms to convert data into mathematical representation. The input to the hash function is of arbitrary length but output is always of fixed length. Common hashing algorithms are Message Digest 5 (MD5) and Secure Hashing Algorithms (SHA)

Private key :Private key encryption is the form of encryption where only a single private key can encrypt and decrypt information. It is a fast process since it uses a single key. This method works best for closed systems, which have less risk of a third-party intrusion. Data can be encrypted one character at a time or in blocks. Common private-key algorithms include Data Encryption Standard (DES). Triple DES (3DES). Advanced Encryption Standard (AES), and International Data Encryption Algorithm (IDEA).

Public Key: Public key encryption contains two keys for the encryption process, a public and a private key, which are mathematically linked. As the name implies, the public key is freely available to anyone, whereas the private key remains with the intended recipients only, who need it to decipher the messages. Both keys are simply large numbers that aren't identical but are paired with each other, which is where the "asymmetric" part comes in.

This type of encryption is useful when many data sources must send protected information to just a few recipients. Public key methods include Rivest-Shamir-Adelman (RSA) Key Exchange and Diffie-Hellman Key Agreement.

Multi Factor Authentication

Multi-factor Authentication (MFA) is an authentication method that requires the user to provide two or more verification factors to gain access to a resource such as an application, online account, or a VPN. MFA is a core component of a strong identity and access management (IAM) policy. Rather than just asking for a username and password, MFA requires one or more additional verification factors, which decreases the likelihood of a successful cyber attack.

The main benefit of MFA is it will enhance your organisation's security by requiring your users to identify themselves by more than a username and password. While important, usernames and passwords are vulnerable to brute force attacks and can be stolen by third parties. Enforcing the use of an MFA factor like a thumbprint or physical hardware key means increased confidence that your organisation will stay safe from cyber criminals.

Data Activity Monitoring

Database activity monitoring (DAM) refers to the auditing of database activities such as database access and modifications in real time. By correlating network logs with database logs, DAM tools analyse and report on database activity, provide evidence for breach investigations, and alert on suspicious events.

Data Activity Monitoring helps to track admin activities, detect unauthorised database access from defined IP sources ,and alerts on SOX and other compliance.

Obfuscation or Masking

Obfuscation or masking removes, reshuffle or changes the appearance of the data , without losing the meaning of data. Obfuscation helps to avoid unauthorised users accessing and reading data. Data masking is data centric security. Data masking are two types, persistent and dynamic masking

Persistent Masking: Persistent data masking permanently and irreversibly alters the data that creates safe and secure copies of data by anonymizing and encrypting information that could threaten the privacy, security, or compliance of personal and sensitive data.

Persistent masking changes the data, but is still viable for use to test processes, application or any reporting.

Persistent masking can apply both in-flight data and in-place data.

Dynamic Masking: Dynamic masking changes the appearance of the data to the end user or system without changing the underlying data. Let's take an example, customer service representatives might not need the entire credit card information and only the last 4 digits would be visible to them, whereas a customer service supervisor can see the entire credit card data.

There are several method of masking and obfuscating data:
- Substitution
- Shuffling
- Randomization
- Encryption
- Key masking
- Expression Masking
- Temporal variance
- Value variance
- Nulling or deleting

Key benefits of Masking or Obfuscation:

- **Protect data from unauthorised access**: Data masking helps to restrict or expose critical data from unauthorised users.

- **Support compliance and regulation**: With access to realistic yet de-identified or pseudonymized data, organisations can comply with privacy regulations—including GDPR, CCPA, HIPAA, PCI DSS, and GLBA—and with data governance policies.

- **Improve Test environment**: With proper data masking, production data(actual customer data) can be replicated to test environment safely, It would help to preserve the characteristics of the original information while maintaining data and referential integrity.

Business Challenges

Rabobank counts on agile software development to keep its financial services ahead of the curve. How could it speed up testing without exposing sensitive financial data and personal information?

Transformation

In collaboration with IBM, Rabobank built a Test Data Factory to automate the process of extracting production data and delivering it to test systems, using pseudonymization to maintain data privacy.

Result

Cuts	Higher-quality	Manages
time taken to prepare test data from weeks to days, supporting agile practices	data enables more efficient testing and development	regulatory compliance and reduces risk by meeting strict data privacy standards

Source - https://www.ibm.com/case-studies/rabobank-test-data-factory-infosphere-optim-hades

Data Loss Prevention

Data loss prevention (DLP) ensures that business-critical or sensitive data does not leave an organisation's network and is not damaged or erased. Also focuses on detecting and preventing the loss, leakage or misuse of data.

A comprehensive DLP solution provides the information security team with complete visibility into all data on the network, including:

- **Data in use:** Securing data being used by an application or endpoint through user authentication and access control.

- **Data in motion**: Ensuring the safe transmission of sensitive, confidential or proprietary data while it moves across the network through encryption and/or other e-mail and messaging security measures.

- **Data at rest:** Protecting data that is being stored on any network location, including the cloud, through access restrictions and user authentication.

DLP is also a way for companies to classify business critical information and ensure the company's data policies comply with relevant regulations, such as HIPAA, GDPR and PCI-DSS.

DLP solutions can also provide alerts, enable encryption and isolate data when a breach or other security incident is detected.

Sensitivity Labels

Sensitivity labels are a means to classify your organisation's data in a way that shows how sensitive the data is. This helps you reduce risks in sharing information that shouldn't be accessible to anyone outside your organisation or department. Applying sensitivity labels allows you to protect all your data easily.

Sensitivity labels appear to users as tags applied to a document or email. Sensitivity labels could be predefined or customizable depending upon the organisation needs.

Network Security

Network security is the protection of the underlying networking infrastructure from unauthorised access, misuse, or theft. It involves creating a secure infrastructure for devices, applications, users, and applications to work in a secure manner.

Network security combines multiple layers of defences at the edge and in the network. Each network security layer implements policies and controls. Authorised users gain access to network resources, but malicious actors are blocked from carrying out exploits and threats.

Flagstar Bank disclosed a data breach that leaked the personal information of 1.5 million customers.
An investigation concluded on June 2, 2022, determined that hackers accessed sensitive information in the December 2021 incident. The

bank said it had notified affected individuals, reported to federal law enforcement authorities, and initiated incident response plans.

What happened ?

Flagstar experienced a cyber incident that involved unauthorised access to the company network. In response, Flagstar promptly took steps to secure its environment and investigate the incident with the assistance of third party forensic experts.

Device Security

Devices like mobile, IoT and laptops or servers are very crucial resources in IT industries and very vulnerable for any cyber attack. Today mostly applications are mainly accessed through mobile devices. It is important for organisations to provide the right protection of devices.

General recommendation for device security includes-

- Enable user authentication with 2F authentication
- Each device should have unique private/ Public key pair
- Update OS (Operating system) regularly
- Avoid public Wifi
- Use Password manager
- Provide Data back at regular interval

Facility Security

Facility security is the first line of defence against bad actor.Facility security is the protection, and the measures taken toward the protection, of a building or other physical location. Facility security planning involves both the use of personnel and technology, but though both are important, the quality, training, and trustworthiness of personnel is of greater significance ultimately than the sophistication of the equipment used to protect a facility.

Data Privacy

In January 2019, Google was fined $57M under the new GDPR law. This shows that even the biggest companies are still struggling with what this means to them and how to incorporate the right security and compliance measures within their business ecosystems.

Data privacy, referred to as information privacy, is an area of data protection that concerns the proper handling of sensitive data including, notably, personal data like name, location, contact information, or online or real-world behaviour, also other confidential data, such as certain financial data and intellectual property data, to meet regulatory requirements as well as protecting the confidentiality and immutability of the data.

Data privacy focuses on the rights of individuals, the purpose of data collection and processing, privacy preferences, and the way organisations govern personal data of data subjects.It focuses on how to collect, process, share, archive, and delete the data in accordance with the law.

Personal information is data about an "identifiable individual". It is information that on its own or combined with other pieces of data, can identify you as an individual.

The definition of personal information differs somewhat under PIPEDA or the Privacy Act but generally, it can mean information about your:

- race, national or ethnic origin,
- religion,
- age, marital status,
- medical, education or employment history,
- financial information,
- DNA,

- identifying numbers such as your social insurance number, or driver's licence,
- views or opinions about you as an employee.

Why is Data Privacy Important ?

Privacy is considered a fundamental human right, and data protection laws exist to guard that right. Data privacy is also important because in order for individuals to be willing to engage online, they have to trust that their personal data will be handled with care. Organisations use data protection practices to demonstrate to their customers and users that they can be trusted with their personal data.

Personal data can be misused in a number of ways if it is not safe:

- Criminals can use personal data to defraud or harass users.
- Entities may sell personal data to advertisers or other outside parties without user consent, which can result in users receiving unwanted marketing or advertising.
- When a person's activities are tracked and monitored, this may restrict their ability to express themselves freely, especially under repressive governments.

For individuals, any of these outcomes can be harmful. For a business, these outcomes can irreparably harm their reputation, as well as resulting in fines, sanctions, and other legal consequences.

What are the laws that govern data privacy?

Privacy law is not new. Privacy and information privacy as concepts are firmly linked to the ethical imperative to human rights.

Compliance with regulations is driving the need for de-identification of sensitive data.

such as the-

- EU General Data Protection Regulation (GDPR)

- Payment Card Industry Data Security Standard (PCI DSS)

- US State of California Consumer Privacy Act (CCPA),

- US Health Insurance Portability and Accountability Act (HIPAA)

General Data Protection Regulation (GDPR):

Regulates how the personal data of European Union (EU) data subjects, meaning individuals, can be collected, stored, and processed, and gives data subjects rights to control their personal data.

In 1980, the Organization for Economic Co-Operation and Development (OECD) established guidelines and principles for Fair Information Processing that became basic for the European Union's data protection laws.

GDPR principles.

- **Fairness, Lawfulness, Transparency:** Personal data shall be processed lawfully, fairly, and in a transparent manner.

- **Purpose Limitation:** Personal data must be collected for specified, explicit, legitimate purposes, not processed in a manner that is incompatible with those purposes.

- **Data Minimization:** Personal data must be limited to what is necessary in relation to the purposes for which they are processed.

- **Accuracy:** Personal data must be accurate, and kept up-to-date.

- **Storage Limitation:** Data must be kept in a form that permits identification of data subjects for no longer than it is necessary for the purposes for which the personal data are processed.

- **Integrity and Confidentiality :** Data must be processed in a manner that ensures appropriate security of the personal data.

- **Accountability:** Data controllers shall be responsible for, and be able to demonstrate compliance.

The Personal Information Protection and Electronic Documents Act (PIPEDA)

Canadian privacy law combines a comprehensive regime of privacy protection with industry self regulation. PIPEDA applies to every organisation that collects, uses, and disseminates personal information in the course of commercial activities.

Payment Card Industry Data Security Standard (PCI DSS)

Payment Card Industry Data Security Standard (PCI DSS) is a set of security standards designed to ensure that all organisations that accept, process, store or transmit credit card information such as name, credit card number, bank account number, or account expiration date maintain a secure environment. Most of these data fields are regulated by laws and policies.

The California Consumer Privacy Act of 2018 (CCPA)

CCPA gives consumers more control over the personal information that businesses collect about them and the CCPA regulations provide guidance on how to implement the law. This landmark law secures new privacy rights for California consumers, including:

- The **right to know** about the personal information, a business collects about them and how it is used and shared;

- The **right to delete** personal information collected from them (with some exceptions);

- The **right to opt-out** of the sale of their personal information; and

- The **right to non-discrimination** for exercising their CCPA rights.

Summary

In this chapter, we attempt to provide an overview of data protection and different components of data protection.

We discussed the importance of business continuity and techniques that support data availability such as backup recovery, RAID techniques, Data archiving, retention and Immutability.

Data security is important against unauthorised access. Data security helps to avoid data compromise situations. We covered some basic techniques for data securities that includes access control, data encryption, data masking, data loss prevention, sensitivity labels, network, device and facility security.

Under data privacy, we provide an overview of the importance of privacy and its basic compliance rules like, GDPR, PIPEDA, CCPA, PCI DSS.

References

- https://www.crowdstrike.com/cybersecurity-101/data-loss-prevention-dlp/
- https://nbold.co/sensitivity-labels/
- https://learn-umbrella.cisco.com/ebook-library/2021-cyber-security-threat-trends-phishing-crypto-top-the-list
- https://www.varonis.com/blog/data-breach-statistics
- https://www.documentcloud.org/documents/22064071-flagstar-standard-notification-letter-06-17-2022?responsive=1&title=1

Ten

Build Governance

A well-designed data governance program provides the right ownership and accountability model to get to the root cause and resolution of data issues.

-Allison Sagraves , Chief data officer m&T Bank

Introduction

Power of data in driving business is well recognized. Data is growing exponentially year by year. Managing and accessing trustworthy data is a major challenge for many organisations. Companies have varieties of data and databases platforms where data begins to store and maintain. Different databases are stored in different places and it is silos. This leads to data duplication, unnecessary cost to the organisation for the storage and additional efforts to data maintenance. Quality of such silos data is also a question mark due to different quality standards and it might not be formatted to solve organisational problems for decision making.

If an organisation has "messy data" it would add more risk to the decision making process e.g. if data quality would be an issue it will lead to inability to derive the right meaning from data. If data has open access to all then it will lead to wrong data update or more possibilities of data breach.

In short, if organisation doesn't have control on its data it will lead to:

- Business risk
- Risk in developing business strategy
- Customer dissatisfaction
- Risk of data security and data breach
- More operational cost
- Data access challenges
- Risk of breaching regulatory compliance

So how does an organisation take control of its data and make it useful? Answer is building strong policies, procedure around the different elements of data. It is the same as HR building policies and procedures to control employees and important resources.

As data comes from multiple departments and different internal external sources, organisational level controls are required on data quality accessibility and security.

What is Data Governance ?

Data Governance is a set of processes, policies and standards defined for the management of information within an enterprise and ensures the effective and efficient use of information in enabling an organisation to achieve its goals.

According to DAMA, which is a global data management community, data governance is the exercise of authority, control, and shared decision - making , planning, monitoring, and enforcement over the management of data assets.

Gartner defines "Data governance is the specification of decision rights and an accountability framework to ensure the appropriate behaviour in the valuation, creation, consumption and control of data and analytics."

Data governance defines who can take what action, upon what data, in what situations, using what methods. A well-crafted data governance strategy is fundamental for any organisation that works with data, and will explain how your business benefits from consistent, common processes and responsibilities.

Let's take an example. You are looking for a specific book, you decide to search for that book in one of the famous libraries in your city. Library is quite far from your place but you still decide to go, as that book is very important for you.

On a visit, you would be surprised to see no one asked you to register your entry or asked for your purpose to visit, library open for all without any restrictions. Now, you are looking for your book but all the books are placed randomly, no sequencing based on books name or author names. It's really very difficult for you to search for a specific book from millions of books. You asked the librarian for help, he was not sure, then you checked with multiple people working in the library but every time you got different answers, what do you do next? With more patience you will decide to find your own way. Finally you get what you are looking for after putting in a lot of hard work, suddenly you realise, book quality isn't good and multiple pages are torn. You would be more frustrated and blame yourself for your decision.

The same thing happened in the business world as well, with digital transformation and cheaper storage companies producing and storing enormous amounts of data. Imagine the above library scenarios, the company has data but not a level where the company can rely on or too many time-consuming processes. When data quality is low, it affects every aspect of a business, from marketing insights to financial planning, and hinders the achievement of important KPIs. It's impossible to make accurate decisions or take calculated risks when data quality is poor.

Data Governance Ensure

Drivers for data governance more often focus on enhancing trust in data, reducing risk and improving processes.

Enhancing Trust in Data

Main purpose of data governance is to build trust in data, especially in how that data is collected, analysed, published or used. Data governance strategy address three key aspects:

- Data Discoverability
- Data Security
- Data Accountability

Data discoverability is to provide the ability to easily locate available data, detect its quality, understand its structure, and collect metadata about data, and lineage information. In terms of security, data governance deals with regulatory compliance, management of sensitive data (personally identifiable information etc), and access control. Data accountability talks more about ownership of data and accountability around the boundaries of the data domain.

Data Access Request and Control

Data access governance is a system for defining how your organisation manages and controls who has access to what data assets both internally and externally and then proving that ownership and control. It encompasses the people, processes, and technologies required to manage and protect data access.

The Data Governance Institute defines data governance as "a system of decision rights and accountabilities for information-related processes, executed according to agreed-upon models which describe who can take what actions with what information, and when, under what circumstances, using what methods."

Data Access Governance is just part of the wider discipline of data governance and data management and can be simplified by being in control of, and proving, that you know who has access to what information, why and when.

Risk management

There are concerns throughout the industry about the potential exposure of sensitive information to unauthorised individuals or unintentional data breaches under the wrong circumstances. The risk of exposing sensitive data is quite high and organisations try to minimise this risk by building additional forms of data protection such as data encryption to obfuscate the data objects. Defining policing around data access and identifying sensitive data assets are other major steps towards minimising risk management.

Data governance provides a set of tools, and processes to manage the risk to data. Data risks include:

- **Data Theft**: As data is generating crucial business value, companies are looking for internal and external data sources to take their business decisions. Stealing digital information stored on computers, servers, or electronic devices to obtain confidential information or compromise privacy is more regular.

- **Misuse**: This is often the unknowing use of data in a way that's different from the purpose it was collected. Sensitive information like personal identified information etc. Data governance can protect against misuse with several layers like establishing trust before sharing data, expiring data access URL or limiting the length of accessing data etc can prevent possible misuse.

> **Uber**
> Uber was fined $20,000 by the Federal Trade Commission (FTC) for its "God View" tool in 2014. "God View" lets Uber employees access and track the location and movements of Uber riders without their permission. As a result of their settlement with the FTC, Uber paid their fine and agreed to hire an outside firm to audit their privacy practices every two years from 2014 through 2034.

- **Data Corruption:** The main reason behind permanent data loss. Most data corruptions occur when a file somehow flips or mixes its binary code (bits of 0s and 1s). Bits are mixed up for many reasons, including hardware problems, software-based issues, and human mistakes. Data corruption often occurs outside of data governance.

Data Quality Monitoring and control

According to Gartner research, "the average financial impact of poor data quality on organisations is $9.7 million per year." IBM also discovered that in the US alone, businesses lose $3.1 trillion annually due to poor data quality. Data quality is a key concern for organisations, and poor-quality data creates significant risks and challenges. Data governance policy type specifies the required levels of "fitness" for the information to have optimal risk and value to the enterprise.

<table><tr><td>

Poor Data Quality at a Credit Card Company

One of the credit card companies created a centralised data repository for analysis and reporting purposes. Every time a customer swipes their credit card at any location around the world, the information reaches a central data repository. Each customer transaction record is processed, translated and transformed into a unified format before it stores.

Due to missing logic in handling NULL values in a specific field, entire transaction records were ignored. This causes an erroneous drop in transactions for that merchant's brand name. This issue was unnoticed for a couple of months which caused millions of dollars in loss to the credit company and more on that pursuing misguided business strategies – costing lost time for all teams, damaging credibility for the data analytics team, adding uncertainty as to the reliability of their data and creating lost or incorrect decisions based on the incorrect data.

</td></tr></table>

Source: https://www.anodot.com/blog/price-pay-poor-data-quality/#:~:text=The%20 Financial%20Cost%20of%20Data%20Quality&text=According%20to%20Gartner%20research%2C%2 0%E2%80%9Cthe,due%20to%20poor%20data%20quality.

An effective data policy enables organisations to find and maintain useful information and reduces ROT (redundant, outdated, and trivial information). For example, when dealing with many data entry points, some data will inevitably be duplicated and/or incorrect. Your data policies should enable your team to eliminate these errors to create a single source of truthful, high-quality data.

Avoid Data Silos for better decision-making

Imagine your CEO has a meeting later in the afternoon, and he needs data for average sales in the APAC region for the current year. The Head of analytics pulled a report from the database and highlighted $6.2 Million in sales in the APAC region, but the CEO feels sales are supposed to be more than what has been highlighted in the report. The CEO pulled data from the finance department and that figure shows $7.1 million in sales instead of $6.2 million. It was confusing for him so he decided to recheck with the sales team. The sales dashboard reflects $6.8 million for the current year. It was totally confusing and frustrating for him. The CEO doesn't know how different departments have different sales figures and whom to believe.

Getting different answers to the same questions is something that is not expected from a company which has a strong buildup process and technologies.

Unfortunately, it is the current reality and challenges of the industries. There are so many companies out there which have different definitions of things and different naming conventions for the same things. As a result, final results differ within different teams in a company.

The primary reason for this different result is Data Silo. A data silo is a collection of data that is controlled and owned by one particular department or group but is cut off from others in the organisation. Data silos creates barriers to information sharing and collaboration across departments. Due to inconsistencies in data that may overlap across silos, data quality often suffers. When data is siloed, it's also hard for leaders to get a holistic view of company data.

Let's take an example If a company needs to know a list of active users. What would be the definition, perhaps the definition might differ from department to department.

- For the web analytical team, any users who visited our product landing page could be considered active users.

- For data analytic teams, any users who log in to the system and perform certain operations could be considered as active users.

- For the finance team, any users who purchase something from our product listing page or paid for annual fees could be considered as active users.

Different departments within the company have different definitions of "active user" and their source of truth is their own data source and own definition of things.

Data governance helps to build common definitions and single sources of truth.

A strong data governance allows authorised users to access the same data, erasing the danger of data silos within a company. IT, sales, and marketing teams work together, share data and sights, cross-pollinate knowledge, and save time and resources. Increased data centralization.

Compliance and Privacy

Data governance is about making sure that the organisation is able to maximise the value it gets from its data while controlling security and regulatory risks.

Data governance involves the process of managing organisational data's usability, security, availability, and quality using the internally set rules and policies.

`Data Governance Frameworks

Data Governance implementation needs high-level commitment from top leadership and executive buy-in. The Data Governance Organization (DGO) consists of key individuals within the organisation. A DGO must have the right mix of architecture, subject matter experts, business owners, data stewards, data consumers and other skills that are engaged in maintaining data within the organisation.

Data governance helps to define a clear charter and directive on each role.

Effective data governance involves the entire enterprise. Large organisations typically designate a data governance team responsible for setting goals and priorities, architecting the governance model, gaining budget approval and selecting appropriate technologies to use.

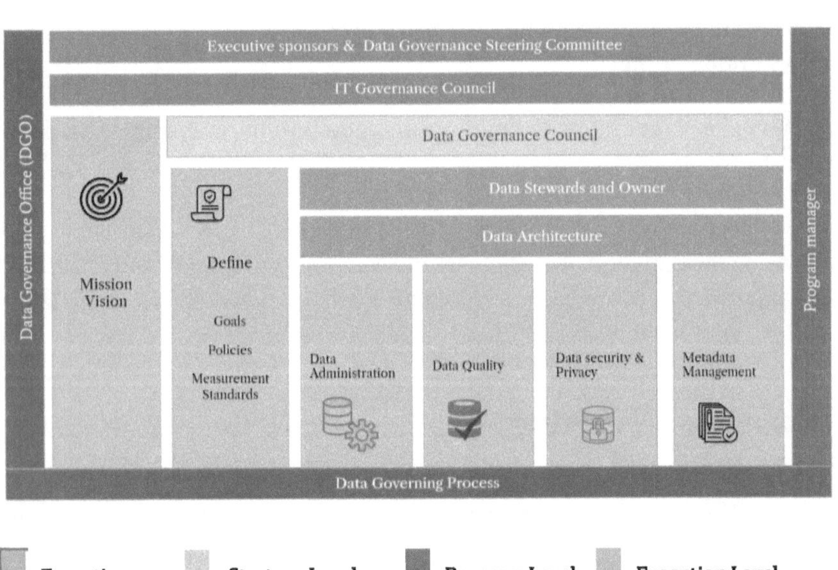

Data governance structure has multiple levels of execution.

Executive Level : Responsible for providing sponsorship i.e. funding and other resources. The executive committee is composed of key executives in your organisation; this can include department heads, business unit heads, and other business leaders (C or V level) deemed essential to successful outcomes.

The executive committee responsible for developing the vision, strategy, and roadmap for their work and have oversight of their staff and teams to drive execution of the work to be done.

Strategic Level: Strategy committee composed of business clients to oversee the governance program. Ensure governance priorities are set and roles include providing direction and overall business strategy. The strategy committee defines governance goals, policies and success measurement parameters.

Execution Level: Is responsible for implementing and executing data policies and procedures into business and various applications. Typical roles include data stewards, database administration , data architectures, subject matter experts etc.

Data Governance Roles - People

Data Stewards

Data Stewards is the aspect of data governance that focuses on managing data throughout its lifecycle. It provides appropriate access to business and IT users, helping them to understand the data.

Data Governance Committee

 DGC works on tactical layer roles. a data governance committee will be established as the main forum for approving data policies and data standards and handling escalated issues. Depending on the size and structure of your organisation, there may be a subcategory for each data domain (eg customer, vendor, product, employee). They also define, monitor, and report on tactical data governance metrics and activities as well as manage the integrity and quality of data.

- Business Data Stewards are business professionals and mainly recognized subject matter experts.

- Technical Data Stewards are IT professionals operating within one of the knowledge areas such as data administration, business intelligence, and Data Quality etc

Data Governance Council

The Data Governance Council (DGC) works on strategic layer roles and is the apex body that internally champions data governance and drives awareness and transformation within the organisation. These individuals set your data policies and provide strategic direction for data. In addition, they resolve escalated issues at a strategic level.

- Executive Data Stewards: A senior manager who serves on a data governance council.

- Enterprise Data Stewards: Have oversight of a domain across business functions

- Chief Data Stewards: May data governance bodies in lieu of the CDO

- Data owner: who specifies the organisation's requirements on data and data quality. They need to be able to take initiative and make decisions for the entire organisation. Their role is business-orientated. Data owners are accountable for the state of the data as an asset.

Steering Committee

Your executive layer roles consist of your steering committee. Your steering committee is the business sponsors who are the champions of strategy and policy of data. These individuals oversee the success of the data governance office.

Data Governance Office (DGO)

The DGO works with business and IT leaders to develop and implement data governance solutions. They also coordinate integration between multiple data governance disciplines as well as administrate, monitor and report data governance activities.

Define Governance Process

The second major area of program execution is a process.

Measurement: Data governance programs should be able to measure progress and success through metrics that would help you to evaluate DG's effectiveness on business values and objectives. Data governance is often viewed as an overhead activity as it is not directly related to any profit generation process. A data governance program is a program of continuous improvement, so effective measurement is a basic component of any successful program.

Communication: Communication framework is important for any big program and data governance is not an exception to it. A better communication framework would ease effective collaboration and expedite the execution process.

RACI: RACI stands for Responsible, Accountable, Consulted and Informed, and is a way of identifying levels of responsibilities in a process, The data governance council is a critical component in a successful data governance programme, as it consists of a group of business and technical stakeholders who are responsible for decisions around the management of data. The results of the RACI matrix analysis create the foundation for the implementation of a data governance council, ensuring that the correct representatives from the business are involved with decisions with data.

Data Governance -Policy

Data governance policy is a collection of principles, frameworks,  programs, roles, and responsibilities that help manage data collection, storage, access, usage, quality, and archival of data assets in its entire life cycle. The data governance policy is usually created by a data governance committee or data governance council. This policy document defines a clear data governance structure for the executive team, managers, and line workers to follow in their daily operations.

 A data governance policy helps employees understand why your procedures are in place, who is responsible for them, and how they should be managed. Drafting this document in a clear, concise, and logical manner keeps all employees and teams across an organisation on the same page so they understand what is expected of them.

While creating policies you should consider the business goal and organisation's needs and objectives. A well-crafted policy should be unique to your organisation's vision, mission and goals. Data governance policy should address:

- Policy Purpose
- Policy Scope
- Policy Rules
- Definitions
- Program structure
- Policy review

Policy Purpose: The statement of purpose describes the reason the policy exists and how it supports the organisation's mission or business objectives. Policy purpose also defines success metrics for measuring the effectiveness of policies.

Policy Scope: The scope explains who is affected by the data governance policy.

Policy Rules: This is the main section that outlines the rules guiding data usage and access.These rules could cover data access (who has access to what data), data usage (how the data will be used), data integration (what transformations the data will undergo), and data integrity.

Definitions: A glossary includes common terminology referenced in the policy. Some examples might include: data, metadata, data access, custodian etc.

Program structure: Defines roles and responsibilities, which are positions within organisations. A RACI chart could help you map out who is accountable, who needs to be consulted, who is responsible and who should be kept informed about the changes.

Review process: Included in a policy by some organisations, this section describes how the data governance policy is established, reviewed, and updated. The review should be performed regularly with the data governance team to ensure that you are still on the right track.

Common Policy rules to consider for incursion

Each organisation has several fundamental policies, most of them having common elements that include:

Data Access and availability: The purpose of this policy is to ensure stakeholders have appropriate access to the information that they need. Policies should include:

- What is the purpose of the company's data?
- Who should provide data access?
- Why is access important?
- How is data classified?

Data Usage: This policy ensures that company data is not misused and used ethically. with consideration for individual privacy, and only as necessary for performing specific roles or functions. The section describes the appropriate purposes and details the common categories of usage, such as-

- Data creation.
- Data updates.
- Read-only access.
- Distribution or sharing outside of the company.
- Consequences of noncompliance, including potential penalties for violations.

Data Quality and Integrity: Data integrity refers to the trustworthiness of the data throughout its lifecycle, including its validity, reliability, and accuracy. The integrity of data can be compromised by internal processes such as human error and unintended transfers, and external forces such as security incidents. The policy should describe who is responsible for ensuring that data is correct and how it should be validated.

Data usability and integration: Sometimes grouped together with the data integrity policy, data integration defines the consolidation of data from multiple sources and provides a unified view across multiple information systems. The data integration policy ensures both the availability of the data and its fitness for use and should include provisions for structuring the data correctly with proper labelling so it can be retrieved.

Data security: While your organisation may have a comprehensive data security policy and framework, including a high-level element in the data governance policy helps reinforce some of these suggested safeguards. Ultimately, security impacts data: Availability, Access, Quality, Integrity.

Data Governance Tools and Technologies

Data governance tools and technologies can form an important part of an overall data governance strategy and implementation as they can automate repetitive activities and processes, enhance productivity, and reduce operational costs. This allows the organisation to scale to the largest volumes of data processing, maintaining the same rules and processes for any application. There are a number of vendors in the market who offer data governance tools with different functionalities and capabilities.

Enterprise Dictionary	Enterprise dictionary is a set of documents of policies, processes or other information. An organisation's enterprise dictionary is normally owned by either the data owner or the legal department
Business Glossary	A business glossary is a collection of data-related terms described in clear language that everyone in an organisation can understand.
Data Classes	A Data class is the identification and allocation of information. A good enterprise dictionary will contain a listing of classes of data the organisation processes. Policies and procedures could be segregated based on the different data classes.
Data Classification	Data discovery and classification tools provide basic capabilities for discovering, classifying, labelling, and reporting the sensitive data in your data. Sensitive data might be financial, healthcare or personal data.
	Data classification consists of separating and organising data based on sets of clearly defined characteristics.
	Depending upon the tags, or classifications it is determined how a certain piece of data should be stored, managed, used and shared based on corporate and regulatory requirements. The data classification process includes
Data	Data consumers either data engineer, scientist or business users who want to access trusted data. A data

Cataloging   catalogue is a detailed inventory of all data assets in an organisation,

Data catalogue is a collection of metadata, combined with data management and search tools, that helps other consumers to find the data they are looking for.

Metadata Management   Metadata management is about managing metadata about data. It gives meaning to and describes the information assets. Metadata unlocks the value of data by improving the data usability and findability.

Metadata management helps to get information much easier and with the right data context.

Data Lineage   Data lineage is the process of tracking the flow of data over time, providing a clear understanding of where the data originated, how it has changed, and its ultimate destination within the data pipeline.

Data lineage tools provide a record of data throughout its lifecycle, including source information and any data transformations that have been applied during any ETL or ELT processes.

Key Management & Encryption   Key Management and encryption is the administration of tasks involved with protecting, storing, and organising encryption keys.

Policy Management   Key management is the process of creating, implementing and maintaining policies and procedures within an organisation. Some software automates policy enforcement and assignment of business rules to ensure full compliance with your governance program.

Business Rule management	Business rule management is a process used to define, deploy, execute, monitor and maintain the variety and complexity of decision rules that is used in various business processes. Business rule management could be manual or automated.
Data Quality	According to Gartner, Data quality tools are the processes and technologies for identifying, understanding and correcting flaws in data that support effective information governance across operational business processes and decision making. The packaged tools available include a range of critical functions, such as profiling, parsing, standardisation, cleansing, matching, enrichment and monitoring.
Data Loss Prevention (DLP)	Data loss prevention (DLP) is a set of tools and processes used to ensure that sensitive data is not lost, misused, or accessed by unauthorised users. DLP is the practice of detecting and preventing data breaches, exfiltration, or unwanted destruction of sensitive data. Organisations use DLP to protect and secure their data and comply with regulations.

Data Governance Roadmap

A Data Governance (DG) roadmap provides a detailed plan or strategy, normally with a list of tasks that must be accomplished for improving or "maturing" a DG program.

Align Business strategy

The first and most important step is to define your governance strategy in alignment with your business strategy. What is the business problem you are trying to solve and how can data help you get there? It happens very often that companies collect heaps of data and later try to figure out what to do with it.

For example, if your business strategy is improving customer services and business growth then your data strategy goal would be more on data quality, exploration, analytics.

If your business strategy is more on attracting new customers then your data strategy is more on digital marketing and analytics on potential prospects.

In Gartner's report, source enhance *your-roadmap-for-data-analytics-governance* explained very well on key steps for data governance strategy and roadmap.

Action to take

Analyse mission-critical priorities and how DG is essential to deliver targeted business value.	Define the scope of governance and evaluate options for deploying a governance framework.	Agree on strategy, align outcomes with phased governance initiatives and show impact on business key initiatives.

Develop Action Plan

Build an effective governance structure

Assess existing governance capabilities and maturity in key areas such as accountability and ethics	Define the operating model for governance and design governance deployment	Set up governance footprints for initiatives and address the need for strategic oversight.

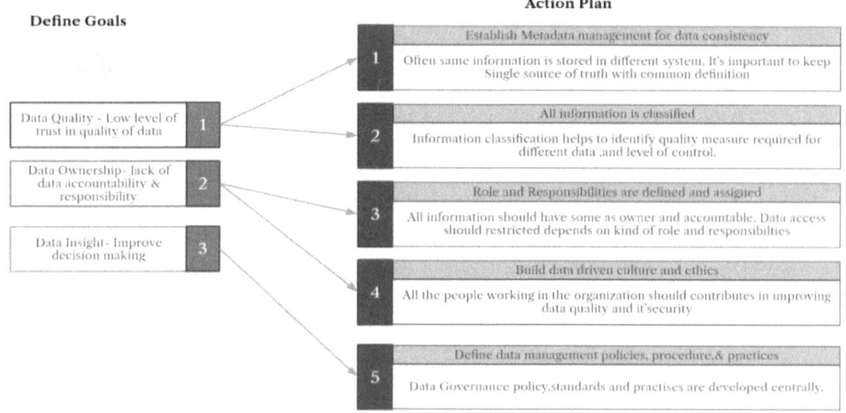

Begin Execution

Design and deploy governance policies and standards

Analyse existing policies and standards and assess overlaps, gaps and conflicts.	Engage with key stakeholders to define the content of policies and standards and assess the deployment plan.	Establish the technology infrastructure, workflows, and compliance and reporting mechanisms.

Monitoring

Evaluate and improve performance

Assess actual operational behaviours and results against expectations, and address issues	Use automated workflow processes and risk thresholds to drive behavioural change.	Evaluate the impact of government policies on business outcomes and identify areas for improvement.

Optimise and Scale

Establish a process of iteration and learning

Track data-related issues and ensure timely and effective routing and resolution.	Devise new enterprise processes, roles and skills plans informed by maturity, culture and risk appetite.	Reassess strategy and model and conduct controlled testing before enterprise-wide launch

Data Governance Maturity Level

A maturity model is one of the most valuable tools available for planning and sustaining a new strategic program. DG maturity model should be customised around the unique goals, priorities and competencies of the organisation. Gartner'S Maturity Model has a total of six stages of maturity.

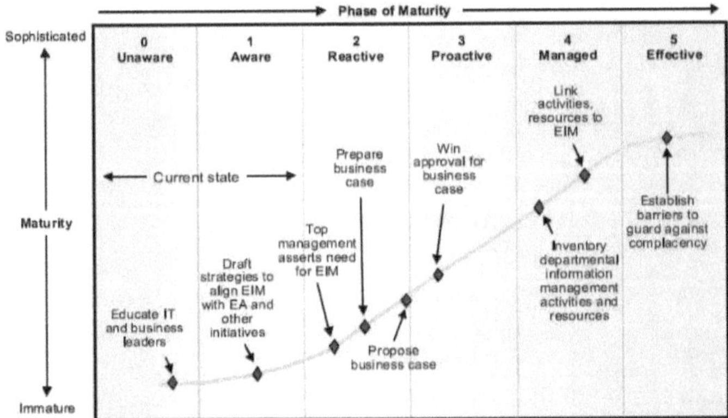

| Level 0- Unaware | • Information/ data governance, security, ownership or accountability does not exist. |
| | • No formal information architecture, principle, |

or process for creating, gathering, sharing and disseminating information.

- There are no common standards, business glossaries, no metadata management, no data models.
- Document management, workflow and archiving mostly occurs via e-mail.
- Information is fragmented and inconsistent across different systems and applications.
- Strategic decisions are not made based on adequate information.

Action items: Architecture staff and strategic planners should educate IT and business leaders on EIM and its potential value. Emphasise the risks of legal and compliance issues.

Level 1 - **Award**	<ul><li>Lack of data ownership becomes apparent</li><li>Lack of business sponsorship in EIM is acknowledged</li><li>The business starts to understand the value of information</li><li>There is awareness in growing data quality issues and inconsistent information</li><li>The need for common standards, principles, processes, procedures, as well as tools and models is recognized</li><li>Business Intelligence outputs inconsistent and redundant reports – Check out this free guide on creating a report inventory</li><li>Inventory and evaluation of risks associated with not having an EIM</li></ul>

Action items: Architecture staff develops EIM strategy in alignment with enterprise architecture and business' strategic intent

Level -2 - Reactive	• Business now understands the value of information • Information is shared on cross-functional projects • Data and information is starting to be shared across systems with different ownership and across departments • Information quality procedures are still reactive • Information management policies and standards are created, but adherence is low • An baseline assessment is developed and metrics are gathered, mainly focused on data and information retention **Action items:** Upper management to promote EIM as the solution for resolving cross-functional information issues. The value proposition for EIM is put together and presented.
Level 3 - Proactive	• Information management is considered necessary to support decisions, and information owners and stewards are assigned to manage this asset. • Information sharing is viewed as the key to enabling enterprise-wide projects. • Governance roles and operating models become formalised. • Full compliance with information management policies and standards. • Data governance is part of every development and deployment project. • Operational risk is minimised. **Action items:** Develop and present the EIM business case to management and stakeholders. Identify EIM

opportunities at the department or unit level.

Level -4 - **Managed**	• Information is viewed as being critical. • Information policies and standards are developed, deployed and well understood throughout the enterprise. • A governance body is placed to resolve cross-functional information issues and identify best practices. • Metrics are refined, information assets are categorised, productivity metrics are developed and shared through dashboards.

Action items: Information management tasks and projects need to be inventoried and ensure they are in sync with the EIM strategy. Create a balanced scorecard for information management.

Level -5 **Effective**	• Information management is seen as a competitive advantage and it is used to create value and efficiency. • Service level agreements are in place. • EIM strategies are tied to lowering risks and meeting/improving productivity targets. • The EIM organisation is well formalised and coordinates all information efforts across the enterprise. • The organisation achieved its EIM goals.

Action items: Implement controls and procedures to ensure information excellence is sustained regardless if the leadership or direction of the enterprise changes.

Data Governance Challenges

Data governance could solve or help to solve a lot of business issues, however, it requires a lot of planning, monitoring and efforts to execute it successfully. Data governance needs a lot of team collaboration, investment and resources which could be challenging in many small organisations.

Data governance is not a business solution which can bring direct revenue but indirectly support handling uncertainty and good data quality which otherwise cause a lot to any business.

Data governance has many challenges to handle few of which are highlighted below:

- **Lack of Leadership**: Business leaders know that for their data assets to deliver competitive advantage they have to be well organised and documented. And without having proper policies and culture it won't be possible. Current challenges with data governance is business leaders understand the importance and values DG can produce but due to lack of visibility or proper vision DG is mostly DG program drag to backlogs.

- **Integration of data governance with IT strategy:** Data governance should be planned and executed under the larger IT strategy. Organisations that view Data governance and IT strategy as separate programs, will struggle.

- **Selecting governance tools**: Selecting the right set of tools and technologies is a complicated and time-consuming job. Select tools based on availability, quality and with trust sources.

- **Organization Cultural change:** Adopting a data-driven approach is a mindset shift and any changes are hard to adopt. Data governance initiatives will bring a lot of ownership, and responsibilities to each individual. Business leaders should cultivate data-driven thought processes in an organisation's culture.

- **Budget and ownership**: One of the challenges that most organisations face focuses on a sufficient budget. DG programs could fail due to a lack of sufficient budget for procuring the right set of tools or people.

Summary

This chapter was designed to give you a fundamental idea of Data Governance. Data Governance ensures data trust, data security and data accessibility. We discussed the data governance framework and different key ingredients of frameworks including people (roles and responsibilities), processes and policies.

From our discussion, it is clear that data governance is not simply an implementation of tools but the overall process and policies. Finally, we provided a step-by-step guide for implementing the governance roadmap.

References

- https://www.pwc.in/consulting/technology/data-and-analytics/govern-your-data/insights/global-and-industry-frameworks-for-data-governance.html
- https://atlan.com/data-governance-framework/
- https://www.varonis.com/blog/data-governance
- https://www.sas.com/content/dam/SAS/documents/marketing-whitepapers-ebooks/sas-whitepapers/en/sas-data-governance-framework-107325.pdf
- https://www.sailpoint.com/identity-library/how-to-build-a-data-governance-policy/
- https://www.gartner.com/en/publications/enhance-your-roadmap-for-data-and-analytics-governance
- https://www.lightsondata.com/data-governance-maturity-models-gartner/

Stay Connected

- **Linkedin** - https://www.linkedin.com/in/vivek-parate/
- **Instagram** - https://www.instagram.com/imdatajourney/
- **FaceBook** - https://www.facebook.com/datajourney
- **Website** - https://www.vivekparate.com